GIRLS ROCK

How to Get Your Group Together and Make Some Noise

Robyn "Sprout" Goodmark
of Northern State

....

ILLUSTRATED BY *Adrienne Yan*

BILLBOARD BOOKS

AN IMPRINT OF WATSON-GUPTILL PUBLICATIONS/NEW YORK

For

Hope, Brooke, Goose, Mickie, Dani, Klein, Red, Cass, Jules, and Spero—all of my ladies who rock; I am honored to rock with you every day. And for my mom, who rocks in a million ways.

Senior Acquisitions Editor: Julie Mazur
Editor: Cathy Hennessy
Designer: Melissa Chang
Production Manager: Sal Destro

Text copyright © 2008 by Robyn Goodmark
Illustrations copyright © 2008 by Adrienne Yan

First published in 2008 by Billboard Books
An imprint of Watson-Guptill Publications, Nielsen Business Media, a division of The Nielsen Company
770 Broadway, New York, NY 10003
www.watsonguptill.com

ISBN-10 0-8230-9948-2
ISBN-13 978-0-8230-9948-1

Watson-Guptill Publications books are available at special discounts when purchased in bulk for premiums and sales promotions, as well as for fund-raising or educational use. Special editions or book excerpts can be created to specification. For details, please contact the Special Sales Director at the address at left.

Library of Congress Cataloging-in-Publication Data

Goodmark, Robyn.
  Girls rock: how to get your group together and make some noise / Robyn Goodmark ; illustrated by Adrienne Yan.
    p. cm.
  Includes index.
  ISBN-13 978-0-8230-9948-1 (alk. paper)
  ISBN-10 0-8230-9948-2 (alk. paper)
  1. Rock music—Vocational guidance—Juvenile literature. 2. Women rock musicians—Vocational guidance—Juvenile literature. I. Yan, Adrienne. ill. II. Title.
  ML3795.G75 2008
  781.66023—dc22

2008007386

Printed in the United States

First printing, 2008

1 2 3 4 5 6 7 8 / 15 14 13 12 11 10 09 08

CONTENTS

FOREWORD BY
Kim Gordon

As a teenager in the late 1960s, my dream was to be a visual artist. I had wanted to be an artist since I was a little kid. I loved music and had boyfriends who were musicians, but I didn't have any interest in making music myself. There weren't many women in bands as role models then. The music I listened to was mostly folk and jazz and avant-garde. I also liked bands like the Velvet Underground, Captain Beefheart, and Frank Zappa's Mother of Invention, who were all—except for the Velvet Underground's amazing drummer Mo Tucker—men. Most women in music were singer-songwriters.

I moved to New York City in 1980 to further my life as an artist, and there I discovered the No Wave music scene. No Wave was a distinct part of the New York punk rock scene, way more weird and artier than the typical three-chord smash. And there were lots of girls in the bands! Many were also artists. So when I saw No Wave bands like DNA, a trio featuring the incredible female drummer Ikue Mori, and The Static, another trio with two radical female players, I really related to it. I felt sort of like: *I could do that!* I loved how the music was less concerned with conventional form and more about expression.

One of my New York friends at this time, a brilliant conceptual artist named Dan Graham, asked if I would form an all-girl band for a performance piece of his. I took the challenge, even though I didn't know how to play anything. The first thing I did was borrow a guitar from my roommate (whose ex-boyfriend had given it to her). Next I had a friend teach me jazz chords by making a half-barre with my fingers across the frets. I concentrated on rhythm. For lyrics, I used ad copy found in women's magazines like *Cosmopolitan*.

That group stopped playing when the performance ended, but one of the women introduced me to a boy named Thurston Moore, and he and I started playing together. Our band, Sonic Youth, has been together ever since—more than twenty-seven years.

After all this time, I still think of myself as more of a visual artist than a musician. But the thing is, it doesn't really matter. Creativity is fluid. Anyone can make music, and anyone can be in a band. The important thing is to find a way to express yourself that's authentic. It doesn't have to fit into any genre or idea of what is feminine or sexy, or even empowering.

One of the biggest obstacles to getting started in music is figuring out how to express yourself while also making something you'd want to listen to on your own iPod. The truth of the matter is that there is no magic formula. Making music is an organic process. It comes from who you and your bandmates are as individuals. The music means something because you create it *together*. It's just as much about how you interact as a group and what you want out of the process as it is about the end product. There are no rules for what music should sound like, just as there should be no rules for how girls should act or dress.

Being in a band is not always easy. You have to be committed for it to work, and ready to figure out problems. And that's just one of the things that makes this book so awesome. Robyn breaks it all down. Even the tough parts. She makes the notion of starting a band something anyone can do. *Girls Rock* is realistic and comprehensive, and lighthearted without being corny. Best of all, it gets you excited about making music! When I read the introduction and its list of reasons for starting a girl band, I immediately wanted to call my thirteen-year-old daughter's teacher to see if I could work it into their curriculum at school.

Every generation of girls deserves a book like *Girls Rock*. It's time to share the secret that it's no secret how to rock. *You* are the magic ingredient.

—Kim Gordon, March 2008

IF WE CAN DO IT, YOU CAN DO IT

Introduction

I grew up surrounded by music. My father and his friends all played the guitar, and some of my earliest memories are of sitting around the living room and singing along while they played songs by Neil Young, Bob Dylan, and Crosby, Stills and Nash. Music was important in my family, and my parents encouraged both my brother and me to learn to play an instrument at an early age. From the very start, my relationship with music frustrated me: I loved it, but every time I tried to get really involved, I felt that I failed in some way. First there were piano lessons that I had to take, while my older brother got to play the drums. I sat on a cold, hard bench for hours practicing the same roots and chords, while later at night my brother got to rock out on his drum set. The piano was clearly doing nothing for me, so I gave up and moved on to something new. I joined the school band and tried to play the flute—but practicing gave me a headache. Imagine what it must have sounded like to my family! Again, I was not feeling it, so after elementary school I left the flute behind.

Meanwhile, when my brother got to high school, he started a band with a friend of his from summer camp. I would hang out at rehearsals in our basement for hours—listening to them write new songs, practice harmonies, and reinterpret older songs they had written. I'd go to every gig that I was allowed to go to—from shows at small clubs in New York City to smelly fraternity houses at nearby colleges. I was thrilled to hear music that I knew and loved being played onstage in public, and to feel the raw energy of the crowd as they sang along with songs I'd heard the band write. But even after years of being a groupie, it never occurred to me that I could form a band of my own. It did inspire me to take guitar lessons, but my fingers felt too weak and I became frustrated when I

SPERO, SPROUT, AND HESTA PRYNN ON THE
STOOP IN BROOKLYN, SPRING 2002. PHOTO
BY KATIE CASSIDY.

could not string the chords together to play a song. After a few months, I gave myself the excuse that there was no point in learning the guitar until I was older and my hands were bigger.

While in college I took a year off to go live in the redwoods of California and to intern at an environmental education center, where I taught fifth and sixth graders about ecology. It was in this setting that I felt confident enough to really learn to play the guitar. All the other teachers either already knew how to play or were learning. It was a supportive environment of creative people who were not afraid to play loud, sing off-key, and goof around. We played simple, three-chord songs to help teach kids about scientific concepts like the water cycle, decomposition, and the food chain. The songs were fun, relatively easy to play, and helped me feel more confident about performing. To tell you the truth, I don't think my hands were much bigger or stronger than they were when I was thirteen, but because of these friends and this environment I finally felt that I could use music to spread ideas in a way that included my full participation and excited me. It was a magical community to belong to, so when I moved back East to finish my college degree, I brought the ideas I had learned with me.

After college, when I returned home, I reunited with two of my best friends from childhood: Julie Potash (Hesta Prynn) and Correne Spero (Spero). Every weekend we would hang out for hours downloading music, dancing around, and acting silly. We had all grown up on Long Island, in the suburbs of New York City, where in the '90s rap dominated top-forty radio. We had seen RUN DMC, Beastie Boys, LL Cool J, De La Soul, Public Enemy, and Yo! MTV Raps, and knew that the powerful new sound and ideas in hip-hop were having a profound effect on our generation. We had watched hip-hop change over the years and had became more aware that there simply were not enough women represented in ways that made us feel proud. We were sick of seeing scantily clad women as background dancers. The three of us reminisced about the music and videos we had grown up with, and we wondered where the positive role models had gone—the Queen Latifahs, the MC Lytes, and the Roxanne Shantes.

Then one night, at a party in 2000, we decided we wanted to start our own female hip-hop band. We thought it was both funny and revolutionary that three white, educated women from Long Island wanted to start a rap band. When we woke up the next morning and still thought it was a good idea, we got started right away. We named it Northern State, after one of the parkways on Long Island, and that was just the beginning. We knew we had to inject our own perspective into a now-familiar genre. We really loved hip-hop and wanted to honor the days when it was used as a political platform for MCs to speak and comment on their lives—but we were not trying to make fun of anyone, or create some kind of spoof. We had to be clever, and aware of our history while creating something new. It was important for us to keep our music light, to entertain people, and not take ourselves too seriously. We have always tried to strike a balance between keeping our sense of humor about what we are doing, and not making complete fools of ourselves. Not easy, but that challenge is part of what has driven us to write new songs and push ourselves to go in different directions musically—and it is also part of what has made being in Northern State so personally rewarding and creatively fulfilling.

In the eight years since we started Northern State, we've had our share of ups and downs. Over the course of recording and releasing three albums, some very exciting things have happened to help us feel good about the choices we have made and the path we have taken. Highlights include meeting and working with some of our hip-hop heroes on

SPERO, SPROUT, AND HESTA PRYNN—WITH STEVE HALPERN ON BASS—REHEARSING IN THE EARLY DAYS AT THE MUSIC BUILDING IN NEW YORK CITY. PHOTO BY KATIE CASSIDY.

the production of our records, like Pete Rock, DJ Muggs from Cypress Hill, ?uestlove from The Roots, and Adrock from the Beastie Boys. We have also toured with, opened for, and shared bills with many artists we admire and have loved for a long time, like The Roots, De La Soul, Talib Kweli, ESG, Le Tigre, Tegan & Sara, The Gossip, and Cake. Most recently, we had two songs from our latest album licensed to the television show Grey's Anatomy, meaning that they played our songs during specific episodes and we got paid for it. Of course, things didn't start out that way. Our earliest shows ranged from performing in our parent's living room, hosting parties for ourselves to play, and playing the same small divey club on the Lower East Side every few weeks until we could get another booking. We've also battled with major independent labels and business managers, had both successful and unsuccessful tours, recorded with lots of different producers, and traveled around for years in our own beat-up cars, lugging our own gear, selling our own merch, and barely making ends meet.

SPROUT ON THE MIC RECORDING DYING IN STEREO AT GOOD & EVIL STUDIOS IN BROOKLYN. PHOTO BY GREGORY KRAMER.

Since the early days, eight years ago, we've also had a few opportunities to play shows for younger audiences at The Willie Mae Rock Camp for Girls in New York City, The Power Chord Academy in Boston, and a festival to raise money for the Paul Green School of Rock in Wilmington, Delaware. Looking out into the crowd at those shows and seeing younger girls getting psyched to start their own bands was definitely worth the wait and all the work.

It's never too early to start expressing yourself creatively, whether it is through an instrument, writing songs, jamming with friends, or learning how to promote and build a project you are proud of. There is no feeling in the world like getting your girls together and making some noise—just rocking out and playing music. Your band can serve as a way to express yourself and develop a creative outlet for your ideas, while being an amazing release for any tensions that are created by school or family and friends. You don't have to get a record deal with a major label to reap great rewards. The most challenging project you have ever taken on can also prove the most fun you will have in your life. Northern State was a way for my girls and me to feel that we could be proactive about the lack of positive female role models in hip-hop. What will your band mean to you? While there are countless artists, musicians, and poets we can learn from and be inspired by—both male and female alike—more of us girls have to get out there and represent ourselves in the way we want the world to see us. Why should boys have all the fun? Start your own band! Start your own revolution: You never know where it will lead.

Robyn Goodmart

sproul

TOP TEN REASONS FOR STARTING A GIRL BAND

1. You are looking for something to do after school.
2. You are looking for a way to harness your creativity.
3. You are feeling inspired by a certain genre of music.
4. You have written a song, or have an idea for a song.
5. You love to perform and be the center of attention.
6. You have a group of really talented friends.
7. You have a great idea for a band name or concept.
8. You are sick of seeing bands made up of all boys.
9. You want to do something original for an upcoming talent show.
10. You were born to rock.

Quiz: IS THIS BOOK RIGHT FOR YOU?

PUT A CHECK MARK NEXT TO EACH ANSWER YOU AGREE WITH.

1 HAVE YOU EVER DREAMED ABOUT:

- ☑ Traveling the world?
- ☑ Rocking out onstage?
- ☐ Writing and recording music?

2 DO YOU EVER:

- ☐ Make up your own words to songs in your head?
- ☑ Hum your own melodies or create your own beats?
- ☐ Write poetry or lyrics in your journal?

3 DID YOU EVER FEEL LIKE:

- ☐ The music you hear speaks to you in a meaningful way?
- ☐ You have something locked inside you that you want to say or express?
- ☑ There are songs that can explain your feelings or thoughts in a way nothing else can?

4 DID YOU EVER THINK THAT:

- ☐ There are just too many bands made up of boys or men?
- ☑ There should be more female artists playing music?
- ☐ It's easier for boys to learn instruments or start their own bands?

5 HAVE YOU EVER:

- ☑ Been inspired by a female musician?
- ☐ Thought about learning an instrument?
- ☑ Wished you could write a song or play in a band?

6 WOULD YOU LIKE TO:

☑ Get up onstage and perform in front of people?

☐ Be part of a group?

☐ Share your ideas and thoughts with people?

7 DO YOU:

☑ Feel like you need practice building self-confidence?

☐ Like the idea of teaming up with other girls to improve your self-esteem?

☐ Think being part of a band will help improve your self-image?

8 DO YOU EVER:

☑ Dance around your room pretending to be a rock star?

☐ Play air guitar and think you could be good at it?

☐ Sing in the shower?

9 DO YOU FEEL LIKE:

☑ You know a lot of talented people who could create interesting art together?

☐ There is a message or cause you want to get behind and work toward changing people's minds about?

☐ There is nothing you cannot do when you are with your girlfriends?

10 DO YOU HAVE AN INTEREST IN:

☐ Graphic design, photography, filmmaking, or clothing design?

☑ Technology, digital recording, or sound engineering?

☐ Marketing, promotion, advertising, or business?

ANSWER: Did you check even one of the answers above? If so, you could be a rock star waiting to happen. Turn the page and get started!

FINDING THE
MUSIC IN YOU

What Kind of Band Do You Want?

Every girl who wants to be in a band has her own reasons for doing so. For me, forming my first band fulfilled a lifelong dream that I never even knew I had. Of course, I recognized parts of it, but it took time to put them all together. I'd always known I wanted to do something special with my life. I dreamed of being some kind of writer and finding a way to connect with an audience. I wanted to be noticed for my abilities and talents, to share my ideas, and to perform in some way. But the idea of starting a band—and more specifically, a hip-hop band, never seemed to be within the realm of possibility.

While you might think that being white and female would make it difficult to start a hip-hop band, those very factors are partially what made it possible for Northern State to get off the ground. In the beginning, when our band was just getting started, it was relatively easy for people to remember who we were. We were "those white girls rapping." We were doing something unique and interesting. It was something to see, something to check out—a bit of a novelty. The difficult part was convincing people to take our music seriously—that it was not just a gimmick or a novelty act that was soon going to fade into obscurity. As "easy" as it was to get started (and I put easy in quotes because it wasn't that easy at all!), we worked really hard and did all the things you will read about, but it turned out to be much harder to keep the band going for the last eight years than to launch it in the first place. The challenge is to continue to write and record music, and to get our message out while having to prove to people that we are a real band— not just some silly girls rapping cause it's a funny thing to do. Three full-length albums later, there are still people who want to dismiss us as a novelty act, a passing fad, or simply "the female Beastie Boys." Even so, we have worked hard to earn the right to defend ourselves as a serious musical force—and a part of hip-hop history.

I started a second band, for totally different reasons. Once Northern State became a job with serious responsibilities, I wanted another band I could be in just for fun or, "for the love of rock." In this band, we usually combine rehearsals with going out to dinner or cooking up Mexican feasts. We play only a few gigs a year and definitely do not take ourselves too seriously. We write silly songs, learn to play covers, and sometimes just "jam out" on the same three chords for hours. We turn the lights down low and rock as if we were consummate musicians, even though many of us have been playing our instruments for only a year or two. It's just fun. No pressure, no big plans—just rock (and Mexican food!).

Don't worry about following the herd: Do your own thing. Listen to as many types of music as possible with an open mind.

—COLLETTE MCLAFFERTY, *EDIBLERED*

What about you? Are you dreaming of a serious career in music, or do you just want to mess around and have fun? Is there one type of music you want to play, or are you open to anything? Do you want a serious band that practices once a week, or a more casual group that gets together whenever? Do you know what instrument you want to play, or are you open to figuring it out later? It's a good idea to think about these things before you start looking for girl members. No matter what your answers, you can find bandmates who feel the same way. And remember—not all the decisions you make at the beginning have to be the final, be-all and end-all of your band. Many aspects of it can change over time.

Finding THE MUSIC in You

The music is the most important part of your band. It should inspire you, spark your creativity, and be the jumping-off point for everything else. You need to be excited about the music you are playing and/or writing, whether it's cover songs or originals, hard-core punk, pop, classic rock, hip-hop, folk, metal, reggae, or any combination. So before you launch your band, think about the music you love and want to play! Here are some questions to ask yourself before you look for bandmates, and then again once you have found them.

What Made You Want to Be in a Band?

Was there a particular video or concert that made you feel like you were born to rock? Is there a certain song you feel so connected to that it inspires you to speak to others in the same way? Is there a band that speaks to you in a way nothing else can or ever will? If so, don't fight it. This could be your *inspiration*.

Inspiration doesn't have to come from just one thing. It can come from a combination of bands, videos, performances, and songs that you love and that make you feel a special connection to music. If you love a certain band or song, it doesn't mean that you have to model your own band on them. It is simply a spark that can get your creativity fired up.

Inspiration plays a big part in many art forms—from painting to sculpture, from songwriting to acting. Most artists speak about things that have inspired them over the years. Perhaps one day your band will be a source of inspiration to other girls.

While your inspiration can come from a variety of sources, your *influences* generally consist of other bands and musicians who make the type of music you want to play, or the style of songs you want to write. What if you don't know yet who your influences will be? Don't worry! Once you start rocking, think about your sound and who it sounds most like, or who you *want* it to sound like. Be aware of those who came before you and acknowledge their influence. As one of my influences and sources of inspiration, the Beastie Boys, once said, "There are only twenty-four hours in a day, and there are only twelve notes that a man [or girl] can play." There is no way to completely reinvent music every time you pick up an instrument! You are going to play notes people have played before, and you may find yourself playing in the style of someone who has come before you. This is totally acceptable. You simply need to find a way to make your music uniquely your own.

The goal is to take the things in your life that inspire and influence you, to mix them together with your personal style and flair, and turn out something unique that other people will want to hear. There is an ever-changing cycle of inspiration and influence. You can be a part of it, too.

⫸ **TIP** ⫸

The musicians you work and play with will have a lot to do with what kind of band you have, so it's important to be on the same page. But you also need to be flexible and allow your ideas to morph and change and be influenced by one another. Ultimately, the music you make as a band should be a mixture of each member's likes, influences, and inspirations—that is, if you want to keep everyone happy and the band working well as a team.

> *Figure out why you* love music and want to perform it, and keep that reason close to your heart at all times. —ELIZABETH ELKINS, *THE SWEAR*

What Kind of Music Do You Like to Listen To?

You want your band to be something you won't get sick of easily, because you are going to be hearing a lot of it. Rehearsals and recording can be very repetitive. Playing and listening to the same song over and over can be difficult no matter what, so play music and songs you love and can get excited about. That said, it is also possible that you like and want to play more than one type of music. Some of the most interesting and innovative bands out there play music that blends different genres. You might hear hip-hop with heavy rock guitar sounds, or pop with a country-and-western flair. These are great examples of putting different kinds of music together in a way that many people can enjoy.

One fun thing that might help ignite your inspiration is to go and see some live music in your town or neighboring city. You will most definitely need your parents' permission, and more than likely, you will need at least one of them to be willing to go with you or at least drive you there and drop you off. You can look online for bands you like and see if any of their touring schedules are bringing them anywhere nearby for an all-ages show. Or you can look at the calendar or schedule of a nearby club or venue that allows in people under 18, and see what kinds of local bands are playing. These days, most bands have some kind of online presence, such as a MySpace page where you can go to hear excerpts of their songs, read their bio, and see what they are all about. If you find a group you like, going to see them play live might be the very thing that helps inspire you to get your band started.

Getting Your Band Together

When we decided to start Northern State, we just knew that the three of us were in it for the long haul. There were no questions in our minds. This was something that the three of us were going to do, and no one was going to stop us. It has been that way for over eight years. Along the way we have worked with many different backup musicians, both in the studio when recording albums, and on the road while touring. It has been interesting over the years to see how different personalities and talents work (and don't work) together within our dynamic.

Starting my other band was a whole different ballgame. My girlfriends and I knew we wanted to get together and play music. We had enough ladies who played guitar, and I was willing to try out the drums, but we needed someone to play the bass. While we didn't know any women who played bass at the time, I knew my friend Andrea might be willing to learn and would definitely be an asset to the group in other ways. I told her about the band, said we were looking for a bass player, and asked whether she was interested. I could tell her level of interest and commitment was high when she went out right away and bought a bass and an amp to practice with at home. She really took the project on and has improved tremendously in a relatively short amount of time—with no formal lessons.

Playing in a band with someone is a lot like being best friends, or partners. If it ends up being a long-term relationship, it will influence who you are and what you do for years to come. To be less dramatic about it, you're going to be spending a lot of time together, so you need to be able to get along and have fun! That doesn't mean you already have to be best friends—playing in a band is the kind of shared experience that brings people together who wouldn't normally hang out. Just like any club or activity, a band is a place for people with similar interests to come together and make something happen. It is a great way to get to know new girls and/or bond with some seriously cool chicks you already know. Either way, brace yourself for the amazing feeling you will have when you finally get the right girls together and start rocking!

It is so much fun to rock out with your friends! Even if you are just learning, you will learn faster if you are playing with other people.

—KATIE CASSIDY, NORTHERN STATE

An average band has three to six members. Four or five is ideal if you are thinking of including drums, bass, guitar, keyboard, and vocals. Six is probably the limit for a manageable group. More than six, and there are just too many personalities involved and problems that can arise.

The girls you play with will have a tremendous impact on the vibe and feeling of your band. The goal is for band practice to be *fun*. You should be able to work hard together, but also to laugh (sometimes at yourselves . . .) and be silly. Some very creative ideas start out as pretty cheesy—and may sound stupid at first—so it's important that the band be a safe space for expression, free from judgment and criticism. Everyone should feel that her ideas are respected, valued, heard, and tried out. Remember: A band is about enjoying your love of music and expressing your creativity.

So, how do you find the right girls? Read on and this chapter will tell you how to get your crew together.

The SEARCH Is On

When you start looking for bandmates, think about personalities that would make for a good band dynamic. The most important characteristics are enthusiasm, motivation, talent, a positive attitude, a cooperative spirit, and a willingness to compromise. There is plenty of time to learn your instrument and become a better musician—more important is the desire to rock and to creatively express yourselves while working together.

Think about girls you already know, as well as other girls in school or after-school activities who might contribute to your band. Your best bet is to find a good mix of diverse talents and interests. It is not necessary for each member to be an expert player of her instrument. Maybe someone you know takes piano lessons, or plays an instrument in the school band. Maybe you have a friend who sings in the chorus. Do you know someone who likes to perform and is not too shy about getting up in front of people? Who do you know that might contribute good energy and creative ideas?

If you can think of any girls you feel comfortable approaching, talk to them in person or drop them an e-mail to feel out their interest. If not, here are a few ways to approach a wider circle of girls:

- Place an ad in your school newspaper or your town's local paper.
- Place an ad online in a community chat room, blog, or social networking site, like MySpace or Facebook.

◀◀ TIP ▶▶

Talk to your parents and get their permission before approaching other girls. That way you can avoid any embarrassment if your folks veto the idea later. And always get their permission before posting anything online!

- Make posters or signs advertising what you are looking for and hang them up at school, the local music store, or any other place where you think interested girls might see them.

Holding INTERVIEWS

If someone answers your ad, or if a friend of yours is interested, set up a time to interview her or hold an audition. Always talk to your parents or a teacher first to make sure there is a safe place to do this with an adult around. Never, under any circumstances, agree to meet a stranger in an unsupervised place where you might put yourself in danger.

◀◀ TIP ▶▶

Not sure when to figure out what instrument each girl will play? These decisions can be made either before you find band members, or after. For example, if you know you want a bass player, look for someone who plays bass (or wants to learn). But if you are more interested in finding the right personalities, focus on that aspect and figure out the instrument parts later. As long as there is drive, talent, flexibility, and a good mix of personalities, it can work either way.

Before you meet, make a list of questions. You want to find out as much as you can about her interests, talents, and availability. It's also a good idea to discuss your expectations and what you both want out of the experience. While it is fun to dream big, it is also important to be realistic about the commitment necessary to make a band happen. If her answers match your own expectations about the band, and you get an overall good feeling from her, then it might be a match!

As you add bandmates, include them in future interviews so everyone is onboard and there are no personality clashes. The idea is not for you to be "the boss," but for everyone in the band to be treated as equals.

GETTING TO KNOW

Here are some sample questions to ask a potential band member in an interview:

1. Why do you want to play in a band?
2. What instrument do you play or want to play?
3. How long have you played your instrument, and how often do you practice?
4. What kind of music do you like to listen to?
5. What are your favorite bands?
6. What kind of music do you want to play?
7. Are you interested in writing songs or learning how to write songs?
8. Do you know of, or have access to, a space where our band can rehearse?
9. How often are you available to rehearse?
10. What are your expectations for how this band would work?
11. Do you have any gear or musical equipment?
12. Have you ever performed in front of an audience?
13. Are you comfortable being in front of people?
14. Do you have experience or interest in home recording?
15. Do you have any experience or interest in photography, graphic design, or other visual arts?
16. How comfortable are you dealing with money?
17. How can you best describe your personality in a time of crisis or difficulty?
18. What are some of your other hobbies or interests?
19. What skills, assets, or personality traits do you feel you can contribute to this band?
20. Do you see yourself playing music professionally when you get older?

TEN GOOD SIGNS TO LOOK FOR IN THE INTERVIEW

1. Was she on time?
2. Did she make eye contact?
3. Was she enthusiastic and positive?
4. Did she bring her own ideas suggestions?
5. Did she ask questions?
6. Was she a good listener?
7. Did she stay focused?
8. Does she seem to have enough time to commit to the band?
9. Did she seem open-minded?
10. Was she friendly?

MEETING OF
THE MINDS

Holding Your First Band Meeting

Once you've found a few interested girls, it's time to plan the first meeting. As you can imagine, there are many things to discuss! It's a good idea to meet after school or on the weekend when you can relax and spend some time getting to know one another. In the future, you may want to take turns hosting band meetings and rotating houses. Whoever is hosting should prepare a snack, so no one is distracted by hunger and everyone stays in a good mood.

It's also a good idea to set an agenda for the meeting, so you can be sure to cover every topic and stay on track. Obviously, you are allowed to get sidetracked and discuss personal business (new haircuts, what happened at school, so-and-so's new crush...). That is part of the fun of having a band! But you do have a limited amount of time, and an agenda will help you keep track of where you left off whenever you do get sidetracked.

For the first band meeting, there are lots of key points to cover. You don't need to make final decisions on these things, but you should at least get the ball rolling to see where your bandmates stand. These key issues are:

- *Your band's identity: What sort of band do you want to be?*
- *What kind of music your band will play*
- *What instrument(s) each girl will play*
- *Your band's name*
- *Where and when you will rehearse*
- *Your basic goals and dreams*

If you get through your agenda and still have time, you can talk about any number of things, from songwriting ideas to dream gigs, cool cover songs you want to learn, field trips to see other bands play, and timelines for the future. All of these will be discussed in upcoming chapters.

First BAND Meeting

Here's one way to plan your first band meeting. Feel free to follow this agenda, revise it, or make up your own entirely from scratch!

1. Opening Circle. Going around in a circle, have each girl introduce herself and talk about her ideas for the band.

- You might want to appoint someone as timekeeper to make sure each girl talks only for a few minutes so that the meeting keeps moving.

- You can go around the circle more than once, asking a different question each time. For example: Why did you join the band? What is your favorite music? What music do you want to learn how to play? What instrument do you play, and how long have you played it? What talents are you bringing to the group? What are your hopes and dreams for the band? Asking these questions will give you a better idea of each member's hopes and expectations, in addition to what aspects of the band each girl would like to be more involved in.

- You may want to have someone take notes in a band notebook. This can come in handy later, so you can refer back to this exciting first meeting and see if there are plans that got overlooked and should be revisited.

2. Find Commonalities. After you've heard everyone's initial thoughts and ideas, go back and find the things everyone agreed on. Namely:

- Do you agree on the type(s) of music you want to play?
- Do you agree on what kind of band you want to be?
- Do you agree on who will play what instruments?
- Do you agree on how often you will rehearse?

THE OPENING CIRCLE

The opening circle isn't just for the first meeting—you may want to start every meeting this way, giving each girl a chance to share thoughts and/or provide a brief update of things going on in her life. This is helpful for several reasons. You get social stuff out of the way, so you can focus the rest of the meeting on band business, and it also helps you get to know each other better. In my band, we often meet at dinnertime and have our opening circle as we eat, sharing news like a promotion at work, a new relationship, or stuff going on in our families. We try to get around the whole circle during dinner so that once we are done eating, we can concentrate on the matter at hand: rocking! Keep your circle moving quickly so that it doesn't take over the entire meeting. It helps to put someone in charge—she can keep the conversation moving, make sure everyone is included, and steer things back to the agenda when it is time to do so. You might want to rotate this position each week so the same girl isn't in charge all the time.

It is helpful to have a chart or big piece of paper to write these things on, so everyone can see them. This also makes it easier to vote, if necessary.

3. **Discuss Differences.** What are the things you do *not* agree on? For each, write the differing ideas on a chart. See if you can take a vote or come to some agreement. If not, you can either revisit these topics at the next meeting or try some of the strategies in the tip on page 17.

4. **Choose a Name.** This may be hard to resolve in the first meeting. But it's a good idea to write down at least some ideas that you can revisit later. Check out chapter 5 for tips on finding a name.

5. **Schedule the Next Meeting.** Get out your calendars and set up a time for the next meeting. If you are ready to start rocking, figure out where and when to hold your first rehearsal (see chapter 7 for more on rehearsals). If not, set up another time to discuss the remaining issues. There will always be matters to discuss, even once you start playing, so you may decide to set one weekly time for meetings, and another for rehearsals. This is especially smart if you end up paying for rehearsal space, so you don't waste precious time yakking about meeting-type stuff.

When we aren't practicing, we like to try to get together each month to discuss goals and such during our band meetings. We keep track of how long it is, what we talk about, and what we need to do to reach our goals. We like to keep an outline for at least the next six months ahead of us.

—JEN MILLER, *ALABASTER*

Future BAND *Meetings*

As you move forward with your band, you'll want to continue having regular band meetings in addition to rehearsals. (More on rehearsals in chapter 7.) While the rehearsals are for playing, band meetings are opportunities to voice concerns, make suggestions, share ideas, and get to know one another better. You may even find that band meetings are so much fun that you want to extend them into other activities like sleepovers, dinners, or Saturday afternoon movie marathons. There are so many activities you can do as a group to help solidify your bond and deepen the friendships that have started.

TEN BAND-RELATED MOVIES TO WATCH AT A SLEEPOVER WITH YOUR BAND

Freaky Friday (2003)

Girls Just Want to Have Fun (1985)

Hairspray (2007)

Jailhouse Rock (1957)

The Music Man (1962)

Josie and the Pussycats (2001)

Rock 'n' Roll High School (1957)

That Thing That You Do! (1996)

West Side Story (1961)

Yellow Submarine (1968)

As with your first band meeting, it's best to have an agenda for each meeting so you can stay on track. Your future agendas will be dictated by the decisions you make as you move forward. Even after the major decisions have been made, like who is playing which instrument and what kinds of songs you want to play, there are plenty of things to discuss at each meeting or rehearsal, such as:

- Choosing a band name
- Creating a band logo
- Choosing cover songs to play
- Songwriting
- Planning a photo shoot
- Creating do-it-yourself merchandise
- Creating a website/online profile
- Making a video
- Planning a recording session
- Planning a gig
- Fund-raising ideas

◄◄ TIP ►►

One of the most important things each girl can bring to the first band meeting, and every meeting thereafter, is a sense of openness and flexibility. As long as everyone's ideas are given a chance, and each member feels valued and respected, there is no end to where your ideas might take you.

Whether or not you begin each meeting or rehearsal with an opening circle, it's a good idea to do at least a quick check-in to allow band members to share news and information. Maybe someone wrote a song and wants to present it. Maybe someone heard about a battle of the bands and wants to enter. Maybe someone else heard of a rock 'n' roll summer camp and wants to share the information. You can always set the agenda before rehearsal, over e-mail or a band blog. Just remember to keep the meetings moving so you can get to the fun part: making music!

I think communication is the key. If you have a clear consensus among band members, it will be that much easier to convey your band's message to the world.   —TEGAN QUIN, *TEGAN & SARA*

THE ROLES
WE PLAY

Who Does What?

Deciding what role each person in the band will take on can occur at any point, either during the first band meeting or at a subsequent one. It should happen somewhat naturally. If the balance of personalities is right, each girl will be able to exert her strengths and gravitate toward her interests. Remember that every job in the band is important, and that not everyone can be that of "first lady." (Although a band of six front women would be an interesting experiment in creativity . . .)

Ultimately, finding the position in the band that is right for you and your personality will be the best way to make yourself happy. You want to be able to show up at band practice and be yourself. If you are somewhat quiet by nature, and do not like to be the center of attention, maybe playing the bass or keyboard would be a good place for you in the band. On the other hand, if you know you need to be the star of the show and like to be in the limelight, you could play lead guitar or be the lead singer. There should always be a certain amount of flexibility in the roles you play—and no one should be forced into a role they do not feel comfortable with. If there is a role to fill that no one is comfortable taking on, it might be a good time to look outside your group for someone new.

Quiz: WHICH ROLE IS RIGHT FOR YOU?

1 YOUR FRIENDS WOULD DESCRIBE YOU AS:

a) The life of the party.

b) An awesome listener who's always there for them.

c) The social organizer: You can always be counted on to get everyone together and keep things moving.

2 IF YOU PLAYED SOCCER, WHICH POSITION WOULD YOU WANT TO PLAY?

a) Forward: You like to score the goals and get the glory!

b) Midfield: You like supporting both offense and defense, without feeling so much pressure.

c) Captain: You like being in charge and having everyone rely on you.

3 AT A PARTY, YOU LIKE TO:

a) Be the first one out on the dance floor.

b) Wait until there are at least a few people dancing before you join them.

c) Try to get everyone out onto the dance floor and having fun.

4 IF YOU HAD TO PICK ONE OF THE FOLLOWING AS YOUR DREAM CAREER, WHICH WOULD IT BE?

a) Movie star.

b) Veterinarian.

c) President of the United States.

5 WHEN HANGING OUT WITH FRIENDS, YOU LIKE TO:

a) Tell them jokes and make them laugh.

b) Ask them about what's new with them.

c) Organize fun activities that you can all do together.

6 WHEN YOU HEAR A SONG YOU LIKE PLAYING ON THE RADIO, YOU OFTEN:

a) Sing out loud.

b) Play the air drums or guitar.

c) Dance along to its rhythm.

. . . .

IF YOU ANSWERED:

Mostly A's: You love being the center of attention, and everyone knows it! With your look-at-me personality, you're best suited as a front person, either on lead vocals or lead guitar.

Mostly B's: You love being part of a team and having fun with your friends! You might be more comfortable on keyboards, where you can play a major role in the band, but not have all eyes on you.

Mostly C's: With your leadership ability and can-do attitude, there's nothing you can't accomplish! Put your skills to work by not only playing an instrument but also being an awesome band manager, keeping the group motivated, organized, and on track.

Onstage ROLES

In Northern State, we have three front women. While we knew from the start that we wanted to be three powerful female MCs who rapped and got the crowd riled up, we have been continually experimenting with our onstage personas and dynamics. At this point in our career, that is, after almost eight years of performing live, we are more comfortable playing our instruments onstage and adding that to our live act. We are still experimenting with how much each of us is comfortable with "not being up front" and playing with the dynamic of what happens when we go "behind our instruments." We do not want our live show to suffer from a lack of energy, so we constantly have to trade up, taking turns pumping up the crowd. Here are the main roles found onstage in most bands.

Front Person. Many bands have a leader, or "front person." Often, the singer of the band is considered the front person because he or she is at the front of the stage, has a microphone, and sings lead on all or most songs. But other factors go into making someone a good front person: Who likes to talk to the audience? Who does all the songwriting? Who's the most outgoing?

> "The most successful artists know how to be good at all aspects of the music industry. To take pride in your craft, you have to know how to do more than write and perform." —EMIKO (EMIKO, SELF-TITLED BAND)

 **TIP** ▸▸

Keep in mind that your band can change over time. The decisions you make at the first meeting should be considered suggestions—once you start playing and writing music together, some or all of these plans can change.

Maybe there isn't a single girl who is the obvious front person for your band. Bands like the Dixie Chicks, TLC, Destiny's Child, and Tegan & Sara are more collaborative, and their members take turns acting as front person. Perhaps more than one person sings lead on different songs (depending on who writes them), or maybe everyone in the band sings and plays at the same time, in five-part harmony. Any or all of these options are possible, and you and your bandmates might dream up something even more unique!

Other Instrumentation. In addition to the front person, there are many other roles in a band. Here are some traditional ones:

- Lead singer (who does not necessarily have to be the front person)
- Drummer
- Lead guitarist
- Bass player
- Keyboard player
- Rhythm guitarist
- Songwriter (could be any of the above or someone outside the group)
- Backup vocals

But don't stick to those roles—think about what *you* want! There are no rules about what band members can do, and anything you dream up is possible. Perhaps all six girls in your band want to play guitar, and you become the first all-girl band with six guitars and call yourselves Six String.... A band can be anything from two girls playing the spoons to a twelve-piece orchestra with concert harp and cello. The more enthusiastic you are, and the more eager each girl is to learn her instrument, the better your chance of getting your project off the ground. While you may feel pressured to have your band conform to what you see on MTV, remember that being unique and true to your interests is what will make people want to hear you. There are no limits other than those you place on yourself.

BEHIND -the- SCENES Roles

There are also important leadership roles offstage. These might emerge naturally as band members discuss their interests and talents and what each can do to help the band. You can also give one or more of these positions to someone with less musical interest or ability, but who still wants to be involved. Is there a girl who wants to be a part of things but doesn't want to play an instrument? What does she like to do?

Having other girls involved is also a great way to expand the circle and enlarge the group. This will help when it comes time to get people to come see you play. The more people involved, the more they can spread the word and the more people you will attract.

Booking Agent, or Promoter. This is someone who spreads the word about your band, so other kids, friends, and family will want to come hear you play. She might be great at finding places for your band to play, whether at a school talent show, battle of the bands, or some other function or event.

Publicist. The publicist works to get the word out about your band. She may get write-ups in the school and local newspapers, and perhaps an appearance on a local radio show or public access television show. The publicist should be someone who is energetic and has good communication skills.

Band Manager. This is someone whose job is to shape the band's future. This could be one band member, or you could spread the duties among a few members. At some point in most every band's growing career, a manager is hired to help the band manage opportunities and offers that come along. In the beginning, it is usually best to self-manage, or work together as a team, to come up with ideas about where the band's energies should be focused.

Graphic Designer. Is there someone in your band who is artistic? The graphic designer is important when it comes to creating posters, flyers, a website, buttons, stickers, T-shirts, and any other merchandise. A logo with your band's name can be printed on anything in order to spread the word. If you can save the logo as a PDF or JPEG file, you can upload it onto your MySpace page, put it on your website, and use it on anything you create to advertise your band. See chapter 16 for more about merchandising.

Secretary. During band meetings, it's a good idea for someone to take notes on what is discussed. Is there one girl who has nice handwriting (or a laptop) and likes to keep things organized? She might emerge as the natural secretary who keeps track of each meeting's minutes and updates the agenda for each meeting and rehearsal. The secretary also keeps track of the schedule and makes sure everyone knows when and where rehearsals take place. The secretary needs to be someone who is organized and good at handling details. She can also help the band reach compromises when disagreements arise.

Treasurer. Who has talent for dealing with money and numbers? You probably won't make tons of money in the beginning, but you will need to spend a little, whether for equipment, music lessons, rehearsal space, or printing flyers or posters. Having your own band is like having a small business, and every  business needs money to keep itself going. Even if you are lucky enough to have your parents pay for things, it is still important to keep track of who pays, and how much, for each project. The treasurer holds onto receipts and keeps track of money spent (and hopefully, someday, money earned). If money is earned, everyone should get paid back what they spent, and the rest kept in a "band fund" to be used for things like rehearsal space, gear, recordings, or even a pizza party!

◄◄ TIP ►►

If there is a girl in your band who is super-interested in gear and equipment, sound engineering, live mixing, and/or recording, there are lots of ways for her to learn more. Many schools and colleges teach audio engineering, and recording studios offer internships where gear heads and techies can learn more about different kinds of equipment. It's great to get involved in the technical side of things!

Gear Head. Is there someone who is interested in dealing with the instruments, amplifiers, and other gear? It's important for everyone to learn how to work the gear, but there might be a natural "tech person" who already has experience and can help the others. If not, this is a good place to ask for help from an older friend, sibling, or adult who plays an instrument. Gear, or musical equipment (discussed in chapter 8), needs to be handled with care and used properly. The gear head might also take the lead in any recording project you embark on.

Band Photographer. Is one girl interested in photography? Every band needs lots of photos for its website, MySpace page, CD artwork, and countless other uses. Some of the best photos are candids, shot during rehearsals or meetings. There is also a time and place for posed group pictures, in which every member of the band is present. The band photographer can also keep a file or scrapbook of mementos from the band, like photos, flyers, posters, and write-ups in the school paper. This way, when your band is famous, you can look back and "remember when"!

THE NAME GAME

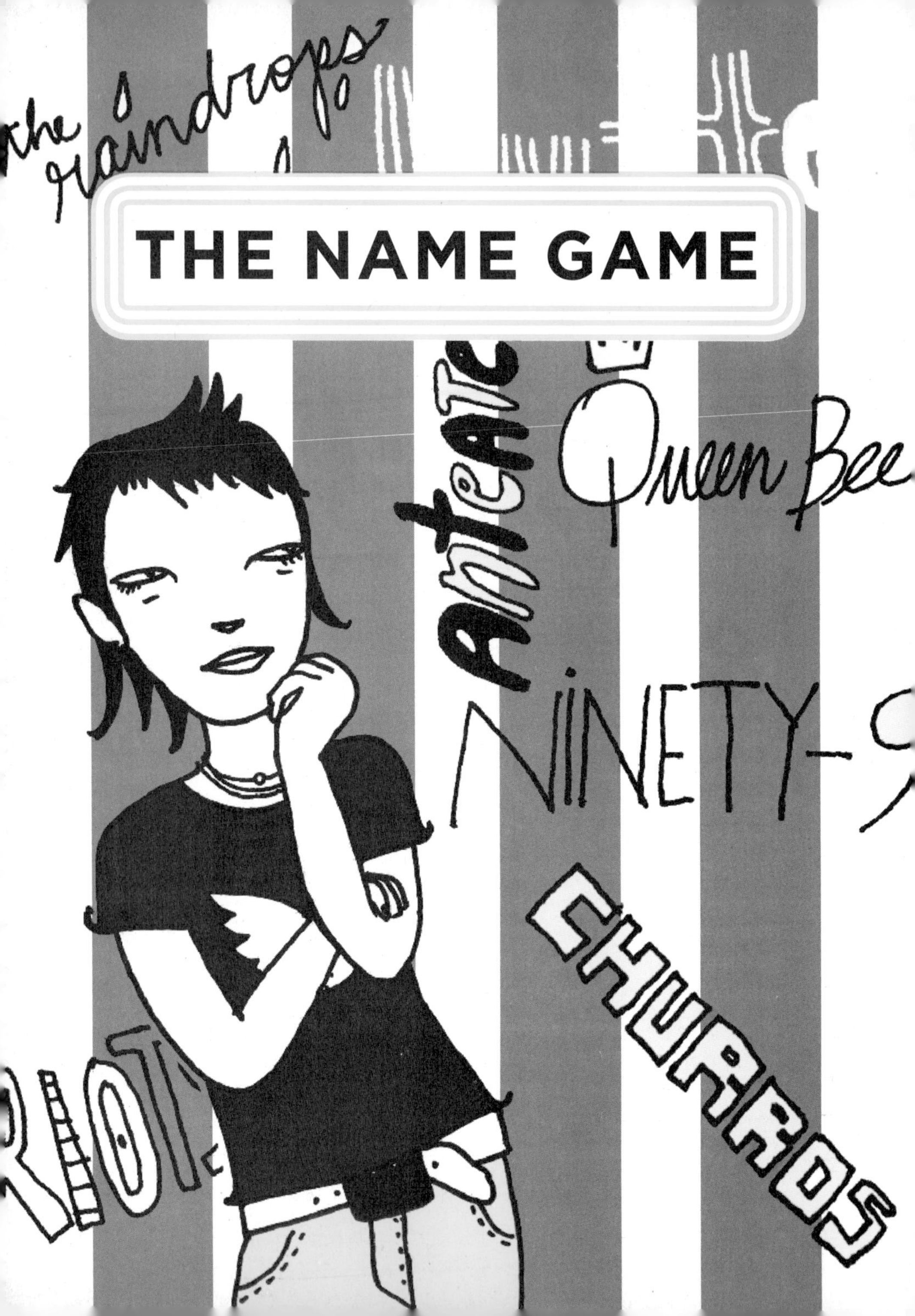

Finding a Name for Your Band

Some people think naming the band is the fun part; others find it to be agony. But one thing everyone agrees on is that the name is important, so consider it carefully!

Maybe you already have an amazing idea for a name. Some bands begin with a great name and build from there, finding band members, and learning how to play their instruments. A good band name can inspire you and influence the type of band you will become. It can also affect how others think of your band, and help them understand what your band is about. That said, you may have everything else figured out—the type of music you want to play, how you will sound, look, dress, and present yourselves, and still have a hard time coming up with a name. Finding a few words that clearly represent a lot of ideas and creativity is a challenging task.

The NAME'S the THING

There are many ways to go about coming up with a name. Here are some of the most common "schools of thought" on naming a band:

It's All About the Music. One idea is to give your band a name that sounds like the type of music you play. An example of a band who did this is Metallica. What kind of music do you think they play? If you guessed heavy metal, you're correct. They gave their band a name that helps people know immediately the kind of music they play. This can be helpful for gaining new fans or getting people to discover your music. If you liked heavy metal music and then heard of the band Metallica for the first time, you'd probably want to check them out. However, if the very same band had gone with a name like Butterfly, you might not have given them a second glance. Other examples of similar band names would be Led Zeppelin, The Grateful Dead, Alice in Chains, Black Sabbath, Guns N' Roses, and the Misfits.

There's No Place Like Home. Another popular strategy is to represent the place you are from. Many band names pay homage to their hometown or whatever part of the country they grew up in. My band, Northern State, is named after a parkway on Long Island that connects the suburbs to New York City: the Northern State Parkway. We grew up on Long Island and have lived in New York City for years and wanted our name to represent where we came from—and have some significance to people. What really happened was that when we needed a name for our band, I was driving back and forth to work looking at street signs and billboards and trying to think of some. I suggested Northern State, among many others (like Strip Mall and Route 110) to my bandmates and they hated them all. A few weeks later, when we still didn't have a name, one of my bandmates asked me what that name was that I had suggested about Long Island and that's how Northern State was born.

Some other examples of this phenomenon include Cypress Hill, The Dixie Chicks, The Mighty Mighty Bosstones (from Boston), and Dion and the Belmonts. If you are interested in this option but nothing comes to mind right away, take some time to look around at street signs and names of places in your neighborhood. There could be a great band name somewhere right in front of your eyes—something you have seen every single day of your life and never even noticed. Be careful not to steal a name from something that is copyrighted or legally protected, like the name of a store or a company. But there might be a way to name your band something unique using words you and your friends are very familiar with and that remind you of home.

Me, Me, Me. There is also the ever-popular style of using a band member's actual name, like The Dave Matthews Band, or Van Halen, or a combination of all the band member's names, like Crosby, Stills and Nash, Tegan & Sara, or TLC.

> **We were lazy and filled out a form for a contest we were entering with just our names 'Tegan and Sara'. I wish we had taken some time to think of a band name. It can be very difficult to change your name once the momentum has started.** —TEGAN QUIN, *TEGAN & SARA*

Something Gr8. Another trend has been to name your band with a combination of words and numbers. Some examples are Blink 182, Sum 41, Matchbox 20, Maroon 5, The Jackson 5, Jurassic 5, 5 for Fighting (five is a popular one!), and 3 doors down. You get the idea.

One-Word Wonders. The trend of the moment (which could be passé by the time you read this!) is to use short, one-word names preceded by "the." For example, The Shins, The Thrills, The Kills, The Strokes, The Vines, and many more.

- - - - - - - - - -

The Right Combination. A *portmanteau* is a word that is created by blending two other words together. One example of a portmanteau is "smog," which comes from "smoke" and "fog." You can use this concept to make up your own great band name. For example, you could combine the words lumberjack and jacket and be called Lumberjacket, or headband and bandit to make Headbandit. There is a band called Japanther made up of the words Japan and Panther. Can you think of other ways to use this method?

TEN QUESTIONS TO HELP YOU FIND THE PERFECT NAME

Here are some questions to ask yourselves that can point you in the right direction when choosing a name for your band:

1. Is there a clear leader of the band who writes all the songs and is the driving force? If so, consider using her name.
2. Do the members of the band have interesting names or names that sound good together? Try blending them together and see how they sound.
3. How many of you are there? Can you turn the number into a name?
4. What kinds of instruments are in your band? Can you use them in your name?
5. Is there a clear sound that defines the music your band will play? How about using that for your name?
6. Is there an image that comes to mind when you hear your music, such as a star or a lightning bolt?
7. Are you trying to express a certain idea or message with your band?
8. What kind of mood does your music convey? Is it hard-core and serious? Is it dark, silly and goofy, feminist or political? Try picking a word that conveys this mood.
9. Are you paying homage or referencing a band that has come before you? If so, try coming up with a unique spin on that name.
10. Is there something about your music or band that stands out?

By the time you read this book, there may be a totally new trend in band naming. A good way to keep up is to pay attention to bands playing in your town, and at bigger venues in cities like New York, such as the Bowery Ballroom, the Mercury Lounge, and the Knitting Factory. You can find these venues online and take a look at their calendars to see what kinds of band names are hot right now.

Our drummer's grandfather came up with the name. He walked into the room where the guys were hanging out and looked at the way they were dressed in their funky jackets, sneakers, and hats (Brandon wore a beret) and remarked that they looked like a bunch of 'new bohemians.'

—EDIE BRICKELL, *EDIE BRICKELL & NEW BOHEMIANS*

More IDEAS

If you are looking for something more "outside of the box" or that does not fall into any of the above categories, try using a random band name generator online. To find one, just use your favorite search engine and type in the words "band name generator." There are several that are easy to use, and most of them are free.

You can also do it yourself the old-fashioned way. Write down random words you like on scraps of paper and throw them into a hat. With your bandmates, take turns picking two or three words out of the hat. Play with the words to create a phrase or combination until you find something that represents the feeling you are trying to create with your band.

Still at a loss? Your best bet might be to give it time. Perhaps after you have had a few band meetings and rehearsals and you actually start to play music, you may have an easier time coming up with a name. If you already have fans and/or family and friends who support your band, try holding a band-naming contest over your e-mail list, band website, or MySpace page.

IT'S
INSTRUMENTAL

Choosing and Playing Your Instrument

If you've never picked up an instrument or sung a note in your life, have no fear: It is never too late to learn. There are plenty of people who don't start bands until after college, or even later. You are lucky to be reading this now. Once you decide what instrument you want to play, you are not far from being able to play it.

The most common instruments used in bands include guitar, bass, drums, keyboard (piano), and vocal microphones. But there is no limit to creativity in music and your band can have flute, tuba, accordion—anything you want!

If you already play an instrument, you should still ask yourself if this is the instrument you see yourself playing in the band. Or is there another instrument you've always wanted to play? If so, now could be the time to try!

If you already know how to play an instrument, and it happens to be the one you want to play in your band, you can skip this chapter. But keep in mind that there is always *something* you can learn about your instrument from someone else, even if it is simply a stylistic change. So keep an open mind and two open ears when it comes to formal lessons or an opportunity to learn from someone with more experience.

Getting an
INSTRUMENT

When I bought my first guitar, I was living out in California, where I had taken a year off from college to teach. Everyone I met out there had a guitar and played some kind of music. I really wanted to learn but wasn't confident I had the ability. I knew a few chords, which I had learned in seventh grade, but I wasn't very good at playing them. So I went down to Santa Cruz, to Sylvan Music, and rented a guitar for $50 a month. This may seem like a lot of money, but it breaks down to only $12.50 per week, just a little more than going to the movies. The guitar itself cost $250 altogether. I rented the guitar for three months, then decided that I loved it and had to have it. I was committed enough to practicing, so I decided I could finally buy it. The $150 I had already spent to rent it was subtracted from the total cost, so I needed only $100 more to buy it outright.

This is called "rent to own" and is a great option for getting your first instrument, especially if you're attempting music for the first time and your parents are concerned about whether you'll stay committed to the instrument or your band. When you rent to own, you get to try the instrument first to see if you like it. You can make sure it's not too difficult, too big, or just not your cup of tea. By the time I got that guitar home and it was mine for good, I had already been playing it for three months—I was attached. And I felt proud to have bought it with my own money, slowly, over a few months' time. Here are more ways to get your hands on an instrument:

Borrow One. Does anyone in your family play an instrument? Ask if there's an old one lying around that they wouldn't mind lending you for a few months to see if you get into it. If you have a piano at home, start taking lessons; if your appetite is whetted, you could look into smaller keyboards that travel more easily (or, the rehearsal space you are renting might come complete with a piano).

Buy a Used One Online. Ask a parent if you can look through listings on websites like eBay and Craigslist. Also, check your local newspaper and bulletin boards in lo-cal music shops or cafés. Always try to see the instrument in person before agreeing to buy it, and try to play it—or have some-one you know who plays the instrument well come with you. You want to make sure it sounds okay and isn't warped or messed up in any major way.

◀◀ TIP ▶▶

It is best to get a parent or guardian involved in making the actual purchase, even if you are spending money you have saved yourself. They can help make sure you are buying something that works, and is reasonably priced. You may think you're getting a great deal, but an instrument that hasn't been taken care of properly can end up costing much more in the long run.

Buy a New One. There is always the option of buying an instrument new at your local music shop. Even if you buy a brand-new instrument, I highly recommend that you first rent something comparable in size, shape, and weight to what you plan to purchase. Especially with a guitar or a bass, there are a number of things to think of:

- Is the size right for your body? Can you hold and carry the instrument comfortably?
- Can you play for a half hour without getting a sore back or shoulder? (This is especially important if you will be playing standing up in your band.)

too big!

- Are you having any trouble holding down the strings? The amount of tension on the strings is called "the action," and some guitars and basses have easier action than others.
- Look at yourself with the instrument. Is it the look you are going for? Are you sure you want that electric blue sparkle?

For the first few weeks or months, practice at home in front of a mirror, playing the chords or notes you know, and consider the questions above. Your instrument is an extension of your creative life. Make sure you are investing your money (or your parents' money) wisely.

> *I'll never forget* the first instrument I bought with my own money—it was a Premier snare drum that I bought at Atlanta Pro Percussion when I was fourteen. It is still one of my most prized possessions.
>
> —KAKI KING *(KAKI KING, SELF-TITLED BAND)*

> *When I was six,* I went to a garage sale with my mom. They had all these Barbies and girly things, and an organ. I was kind of a tomboy and hated dolls, so I chose the organ. —BIANCA MONTALVO, *HEIST AT HAND*

WHICH INSTRUMENT MATCHES YOUR PERSONALITY?

Drummers: Must have good timing and be reliable, dependable, and loyal.

Bass players: Can be quiet and reserved, possibly mysterious.

Guitar players: Often showy and charismatic, sometimes a bit moody.

Keyboard players: Must have long fingers, can be quiet and reserved, but secretly the life of the party.

Learning TO Play

There are many simple songs you can play (or you can even write your own) while knowing only a few notes or chords. "Jamming" is something musicians do to gain proficiency on their instruments and hopefully to stumble on a catchy melody or rhythm (more about that in chapter 9). For now, rest assured that if rocking is what you want to do, you are very, very close to your goal. Here are a few ways to get lessons:

Play at School. If you are lucky, your school may have some kind of music program you can get involved in, whether of the band, orchestra, chorus, or jazz variety. You might receive small-group instruction, or even one-on-one lessons.

Pay for Lessons. Visit your local music store and ask if they have contact information for professional musicians living in your community who offer lessons. Just be aware that these lessons (and the instrument) will cost money, so speak with your parents first and be sure you can commit to practicing before you start.

Trade Your Services. Find a family friend or sibling who plays an instrument and is willing to give you lessons for a discounted "friends and family" rate or for some kind of trade. Perhaps you have a neighbor who plays the bass and can give you lessons while you rake leaves or shovel snow for him or her. Watering plants and mowing the lawn are other services you could offer.

Find a Mentor. You may also find the rare musician who is excited by your interest and willing to become your mentor for no charge. This could be a family member or friend, or even someone your own age who has already taken lessons and can get you started. At some point, you may still want to invest in proper lessons with a more experienced professional, but any opportunity to learn a few notes, chords, or techniques is one you should take. Sometimes it takes only a few moments of inspiration to unlock your inner talents and kick off a lifetime of musical discovery.

> **My parents forced me to play piano, and I hated it. They made me practice thirty minutes a day until I was thirteen, when they let me quit piano and switch to electric guitar. Of course, now I am eternally grateful. Even though I play guitar in my band, I still use the piano to write songs.**
>
> —SANDRA LILIA VELASQUEZ, *PISTOLERA*

ROCK YOUR SUMMER

Rock camps are another fabulous resource for girls who want to rock. The first one was started in Portland, Oregon, but since then, many more have been springing up all over the country. The camps take place in summer and last a week or longer. Most are day camps, though some will find host families for students coming from farther away. Most of them cost money, though some provide financial aid for those who need it.

Rock camps provide instruments and beginning lessons for girls who have never picked up an instrument. The camps include workshops, rehearsals, lessons, and performances by professional female musicians. Like all summer camps, rock camp offers the chance to bond with others and build special skills and self-confidence; it is even more exciting because it also empowers you to rock! In the course of a week, you form bands, name your band, and practice together to play a few songs. There are often performances at the end of the week and opportunities to learn from professional female musicians and from one another. To learn more, check out our list of rock camps on page 176.

Practice MAKES... Better!

No matter how you learn, the most important way to get better is to practice. Once you get the band going, you'll have rehearsals, where you'll all get together to play, but before (and even after) that time, you need to practice by yourself to get your "chops up" so you can be ready for whatever challenges come your way.

Some people find that a regular routine is helpful in any kind of practice, whether it's doing yoga every morning or meditating every night before bed. Try to find a time to practice your instrument at least three times a week for thirty to forty-five minutes per session, maybe after dinner, once you have finished your homework, or right after school, before you start your homework. Practicing every day after school for a half hour is also a great way to clear your mind of the day's stress.

◀◀ TIP ▶▶

Did you know that learning to play music can improve your critical thinking, math and reading abilities, self-esteem, and even your SAT scores?

There are, of course, going to be days when you can't practice or have to stray from your routine. That is all fine and to be expected. But it's important not to let too much time go by between practice sessions. Even if it's too late at night to play your instrument out loud, picking it up and simply placing your fingers on the notes or reading the sheet music and playing it in your head will help you gain musical muscle and brain power.

REHEARSING
THE PARTS

Planning Your First Rehearsal

So you've assembled a group, had a band meeting or two, chosen your instrument, and you're ready to start playing. What next? It's time to plan your first rehearsal. Not only do you need to practice on your own at home, but every band needs to practice together. This chapter will give you the scoop on setting up a great rehearsal.

When Northern State first started rehearsing, we were able to get together at one another's houses, where we would share our rhymes and play around with beats on our computers using different beat-making programs. We didn't bother to set up microphones or amplify the sounds we were using because we didn't need anything to be that loud. We definitely didn't want to disturb our neighbors. Once we started adding live instruments, we realized that we had to find someplace to go where we could set up and play more loudly.

One of the first live drummers we played with lived in an apartment on Flatbush Avenue in Brooklyn, right above Mooney's Pub. Because it was a bar and usually had loud music playing, we were able to set up and play in the apartment and it didn't seem to bother anyone. We spent a lot of time in that apartment playing our songs over and over again, adding live guitar, bass, and drums. It was such a fun environment that we always ended up hanging out for hours. Right across the street, on the second floor, was a gym. I would spend hours sitting on the couch at our drummer's apartment, talking about music, writing songs, and looking across the way at all the people working out on treadmills and stair climbers. Eventually, my guilt got the best of me, and I caved in and joined the gym myself. I would go and work out for a few hours a couple of times a week and I could see our drummer, Seth, hard at work in his apartment, practicing the drums. I would try to make a plan to combine the two activities and work out after band practice . . . or vice versa.

Finding A PLACE

You need a place where you can play your music loudly without disturbing family members or neighbors, and that is convenient for everyone to get to. Here are some ideas:

Rehearsing at Someone's Home. It is possible there is someone in the band who has parents that will allow you to rehearse in their basement or garage during certain hours when they are not home, or while they are busy vacuuming or doing some other chore that is not interrupted by the sound of a band rehearsing. This option is great because it's free, but note that you'll have to bring in all your gear, and set up your own amps and some kind of public-address (PA) or sound system.

If you are able to find a free place to rehearse, it is best to set up your gear once and leave everything there—as long, that is, as it is a safe environment for valuable equipment that can be locked up, protected from theft and from possible damage from the elements. For instance, in anyone's basement, attic, or garage, you will need to make sure that water isn't able to seep through the floor in the case of heavy rain or flooding, which can damage or possibly destroy your expensive instruments and electrical equipment. Another investment to consider is buying some

TIPS ON FINDING A REHEARSAL SPACE

1. Do an online search for music rehearsal spaces in your town or city. You should be able to find a few places to call and ask about prices and what the space includes. Some will even have photos online of what the rehearsal rooms look like and the gear that will be provided.

2. Ask at a local music shop for nearby rehearsal spaces with hourly rentals. Some places will offer only monthly rentals, which may not be practical when you are just starting out.

3. Place an ad in the school or local paper stating what you are looking for in terms of a rehearsal space. Possibly someone in your neighborhood, or a friend of the family, will have a space they wouldn't mind lending out—for the love of rock . . . or for a small fee.

relatively inexpensive foam insulation for the walls to help absorb sound and soundproof the room, if you are trying not to disturb nearby neighbors or parents who are kind enough to let you rehearse.

Renting Rehearsal Space. If you can't find a free place to rehearse, you will have to find a place to rent that you can all get to. Many cities and towns offer hourly rehearsal spaces that are outfitted with gear, and the money you pay to rent the space includes use of the amps, sound system, house drum kit, and microphones. The hourly fee can range from as low as $10 to as much as $50 or more, depending on where the space is located, how big it is, and what kind of equipment is provided. No matter where you live, you should be able to find a space large enough for you to set up and rehearse at a fairly affordable rate. If there are five people in your band, and you rehearse for two hours at $15 per hour, it will end up costing each band member $6 per rehearsal.

◀◀ TIP ▶▶

If you are renting rehearsal space by the hour, time is money! Don't waste time discussing things instead of playing music. It's better to also have a weekly band meeting somewhere else, where you can talk things through, work on lyrics and arrangements, and resolve disagreements before you pay to be in a rehearsal space.

One big advantage to renting space is that you don't have to bring all your gear with you to rehearse. It might be easier to leave your amp set up at home and just bring your guitar to the rehearsal space, and use the amp provided there.

You may also be able to rent a space monthly, in which case you pay a certain amount of money and the space is yours for the whole month to use whenever you want, for as long as you like (instead of paying per hour). If so, you might be able to use the space as a practice room in between scheduled rehearsals. You also have the option of sharing a monthly space with another band or bands and creating a rehearsal schedule so that everyone gets access to the room based on the amount of money they pay toward the rent.

Scheduling REHEARSALS

This brings us to the ever-important question of scheduling rehearsals—not always an easy thing to negotiate. We are busy girls, after all. We all have other commitments and activities that demand our attention, from homework to sports to clubs. One of the main things a band has to commit to is some kind of schedule.

Whether you decide to meet once a week on whatever night is convenient for everyone, or three times a week on the same nights every week, you need to be in constant communication and committed to the schedule, but also flexible and understanding of fellow band members' outside commitments. You may need to say no to other social engagements that arise, and sometimes you will have to compromise because others have commitments they cannot break. Family obligations, religious engagements, homework, and school requirements—these things will often have to come first. It's important to be respectful of the other members' needs and to stay in communication so you can schedule and reschedule rehearsal time as necessary. This is especially important if you are paying for rehearsal space by the hour. Often you have to pay a deposit

in advance to reserve the space—if you have to cancel at the last minute because a band member can't make it, you will still have to pay for the time or lose at least half of your money.

It may be easiest if one band member takes on the thankless job of managing the schedule. This should be someone who is very patient, organized, and can develop and maintain some kind of system, whether a handwritten calendar, an e-mailable spreadsheet, or some kind of online calendar that all band members can gain access to, to keep track of when band members are available. She might keep this information on a Web page or blog so that band members can log on at any time, see one another's schedules, and be able to say, "It looks like we can all rehearse next Wednesday night." Sending e-mails to double-check before booking a space or rescheduling is also a good idea. Remember that often band members will have to check with parents about getting rides to and from rehearsals and making sure there are no other conflicts. Scheduling definitely requires patience and flexibility!

In the beginning I recommend finding at least one day per week that you can hold open for a weekly band meeting and/or rehearsal. If everyone can commit to at least that, you can always add to it from there. It is also a good way to judge the level of commitment from each band member. If certain band members are constantly canceling at the last minute or not showing up, that is a good indication they are not serious about the project. It might be time to call a band meeting to discuss everyone's level of commitment and make sure you are all on the same page.

Setting REHEARSAL Agendas

A good way to stay focused on your task is to set an agenda for each rehearsal or band meeting. This can be done at the end of the previous meeting, or via e-mail between rehearsals. You can even do it during recess or a free period at school if every band member is present. If not, whoever is there can suggest an agenda and then e-mail it around to the other girls, who can add items they want to work on or discuss. It can be one girl's job to print out the agenda and bring it to the next meeting or rehearsal.

Each agenda should include the tasks you want to accomplish at the rehearsal, which songs you are planning to learn or practice, and who is leading or presenting a new song to the group. Whoever has written a new song, or is bringing a new cover song to learn, should come prepared with sheet music, chords, lyrics, and even an audio recording of the song or demo you have made at home to show the other band members, if possible.

I record home demos on my laptop. I make MP3s and send them to the rest of the band. That way, we show up to rehearsal and everyone already knows the songs. Then everyone adds their thing and we work on the arrangement together.

—SANDRA LILIA VELASQUEZ, *PISTOLERA*

GETTING IN GEAR

What You Need to Get Heard

When we started out, we didn't know very much about equipment, but we did know that the most important piece of gear for an MC is a microphone. We also knew that when we performed live, we would want to be able to move around onstage and not get all tangled up in microphone wires. Before we played our first gig, we went to Sam Ash and bought three wireless microphones so we would be able to move around onstage while rapping. They cost about $500 each, which seemed like a lot of money to invest in our band at the very beginning, but the amazing thing is that we are still using the same mics to this day (we've replaced a few parts and had a few repairs done over the years). Buying those microphones now seems like the best investment we could have made in our band, but at the time it seemed like we were taking a huge leap of faith.

The most important *gear,* or equipment, you will need for your band is your instrument (see chapter 6). But instruments are only the beginning! This chapter gives you the lowdown on all the other gear you'll need for your band.

Amps

Everyone but the drummer will need an amp—so they can be heard over the drummer! "Amp" is short for "amplifier": This is a piece of equipment that you plug into an instrument to *amplify* it, or make it louder.

There are different kinds of amps for guitars, basses, and keyboards. And within those groups there are further differentiations as to size, how the amps are set up, and what makes them work. In the beginning, you probably want to start with something basic and not too loud. You also want one that will last a long time, even if you have to move it back and forth between rehearsal space and home. Moving an amp is not easy, as they are usually both heavy and fragile. You can also consider buying a very tiny amp for practicing at home and then leaving your bigger amp at the rehearsal space, if that is appropriate—and you think it is safe. Or, consider practicing at home without an amp (acoustic style, or "unplugged") and leaving your amp where you rehearse.

The main thing to know about amps is that some come in two parts and some are all-in-one, also known as integrated. An all-in-one or "combo" amp has the speaker cabinet, knobs, and plugs (or head) all in the same piece of equipment. You just plug the amp into an outlet and plug your instrument into the amp. Turn it on, raise the volume, adjust the different settings, and you're ready to play.

Other amps come in two or more parts. You attach the "head" to the speaker cabinet (or "cab") using a cable. This kind of amp is usually more expensive and complicated. The one advantage is that the head is smaller and easy to transport, while the speakers, or "cabs," are the large part and often interchangeable. This means you can carry your amp head from home to your rehearsal or gig and just plug it into a waiting cab, without lugging the whole giant amp around. However, the separate head, though smaller, is often still heavy and very fragile.

bass amp "head"

For now, a combo amp is definitely sufficient. This information is meant so that if you come in contact with what I am describing, you can speak as an informed professional and say things like, "Is there a bass amp provided at the venue? Is it a combo amp, or do I need to bring my own head to use with your cab?"

bass amp "cab" →

Cables AND Cords

If you are planning to use amps, you will need cables and cords. Here are the basic ones:

¹/₄-INCH CABLES are used to plug guitars, basses, and keyboards into amps (among other peripherals). They are called ¹/₄-inch cables because on either end they have a plug that fits into a ¹/₄-inch connection.

¹/₄" cable

XLR CABLES are used with microphones. Most microphones have a wire coming out the bottom with a three-pronged end that fits into an XLR cable. XLR cables have two different ends: The "male" end has three prongs sticking out, and the "female" end has three holes into which the prongs can fit.

XLR cable

XLR TO ¹/₄-INCH-INCH CABLES have one end that is XLR (either male or female) and the other end is ¹/₄-inch.

Adaptors attach to the end of ¹/₈-inch cables to accommodate them to a bigger ¹/₄-inch size, so you can plug your headphones into an amp or mixer that only has ¹/₄-inch "ins," or *inputs*.

The PA

Once you have your instruments and amps and it's time to set up and play, you will probably find that it's hard to hear the vocals over all the instruments. This is when a PA system comes into play.

A PA system (short for "public address") is there to make anything that isn't using an amp louder. It is really an amp for the vocals and any other device that doesn't plug into an amp. A PA usually consists of two large speakers and a mixing console with a certain number of inputs, or channels. You plug microphones into the inputs to be heard through the

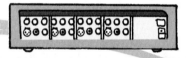

PA system

When I decided I wanted to try being a professional musician, I realized I knew virtually nothing about gear. I enrolled in IAR, which is an audio engineering school in New York City. It was a nine-month program and I went part-time, while working. When you are a female working in music, some professionals may assume that you know nothing about gear, and I thought it was important that I be able to conduct myself in a semi-knowledgeable way. Going to that school was one of the best things I think I ever did.

—SPERO, *NORTHERN STATE*

speakers. You will need at least as many inputs/channels as microphones you plan to use. So if your band has four members, and all four are going to be singing into microphones, you will need a mixer with at least four channels.

Most mixers have a combination of XLR and $\frac{1}{4}$-inch inputs. Some even have regular RCA inputs, which use the kind of cables you see going into your television or DVD player, with red and yellow plugs on the ends. RCA inputs can be used if you want to plug a CD player (or CDJ-type machine, which simulates vinyl records using CDs) or any other type of device into your mixer to play through the speakers. But note that it is not recommended that you plug guitars or basses directly into the PA, as it will be too loud for everyone and difficult to hear one another.

If you are renting a rehearsal space outfitted for bands, there will probably be a PA system of some kind already set up and someone who works there who can help you arrange your equipment and plug everything in, adjusting levels so everyone can hear one another and themselves. This is often a difficult challenge, depending upon where you are playing and what instruments you are using. You don't want to all be playing at your loudest so everyone has to shout to be heard above the music. Instead, you want to find comfortable levels where everyone can hear the vocals and each instrument.

I barely knew how to play guitar when I got started. The trick for me was getting to know and learning from people that were better or more experienced than I was . . . and lots of trial and error. Don't be afraid to not know something and ask questions! —DANI LINNETZ, *THE INKLINGS*

Monitors are used during rehearsals and performances to help improve the quality of the sound onstage. They are simply extra speakers connected to the PA system and set up in different parts of the rehearsal space (or onstage during a performance) so that band members can hear the vocals and other instruments more clearly. Each monitor can have a separate "mix," meaning that each instrument or vocal mic can be louder or softer in each monitor. A sound engineer at a rehearsal space or venue can help determine the appropriate levels during what is known as a *sound check*. Often, the drummer needs a separate monitor or "drum wedge" on the floor behind her with vocals, and maybe guitar and/or bass, playing from it so she can hear them above her own playing. Drums are loud no matter how you slice it. A good drummer will learn to regulate her playing to fit the music the band is making without dominating the overall blend.

The main function of the PA system and amps at rehearsal are for band members to be able to hear themselves and one another. This is critical for playing well together and listening for cues as to tempo, key, and so on. Once you start performing, whether in your living room or at a larger-scale battle of the bands at school, you'll also have to worry about the audience being able to hear all the instruments and vocals. In a larger venue there should be two separate "mixes"—one for the audience and one for onstage. If there is only one PA, and it is directed out toward the audience, it can be difficult for bands to play well because suddenly they cannot hear one another the way they are used to during rehearsal. This is when monitors come in handy—and a good sound engineer.

Here is one way to set up your band for a rehearsal, showing where to put the PA and monitors.

Stage Plot

audience

PA speakers

Smoke Machine

Smoke Machine

wedge

keyboard

guitar amp

monitor wedges

bass amp

drum riser

drum wedge

PA speakers

back of stage

TIME TO ROCK

How to Start Making Music Together

Once you've figured out which instruments each girl will play, you need to start thinking about what music you want to play. It's best to discuss this before your band gets into a rehearsal space for the first time.

There are lots of ways to have fun playing together and interacting with your instruments. There is no one "right" way. Be creative and use your imagination. The more exciting and fun you make each rehearsal, the more inspired you and the others will be to go home and practice on your own, to come back with new ideas, and to make your music even better.

Jamming

One fun way to start playing together is with a good old-fashioned jam session. To "jam" means to play a short, free-form, improvisational piece of music, as opposed to a song that has already been written or played before.

An easy way to jam is to pick three basic *chords*, or group of notes, that everyone can play. Instead of playing an actual song with a beginning, middle, and end, you just play the same three chords in some kind of order, or *progression*. For instance, if everyone knows how to play G, C, and D, you might decide to play those three chords in that order for a specific amount of time. Say you decide to play each chord for two bars, or two counts of four. First, everyone plays the G chord for two bars ("One, two, three, four. Two, two, three, four"). Then, everyone switches at the same time to the C chord, and plays that for two bars, and then to the D chord.

Jamming like this gives you the feeling of playing together, even if you don't know any songs yet. You might even find that after you go around the cycle a few times, you are ready to change the order of the chords, or even to skip one and stay on G and D for four bars each (sixteen counts).

Each time you stop and start over with a new plan for what you want to play and how you want to play it, you will be learning to communicate as a band. You may even find that you don't have to stop to change your plan

I have always loved all kinds of music if I sensed an authentic expression in the mix. Something had to feel real, and that has been my approach to singing. I sing what I feel, and a style emerges from the authenticity of the feeling.   —EDIE BRICKELL, *EDIE BRICKELL & NEW BOHEMIANS*

for what you want to play. Many bands are able to communicate using eye contact, facial expressions, and body language to show when it is time to change to a different part of the song, whether that means switching to the next chord, speeding up or slowing down, getting louder and more rockin', or slowing down and playing more softly. These qualities are called *dynamics*, because they change the way a song comes out so that the same three chords won't sound boring despite being played over and over again. You'd be surprised how many songs have been written with those same three chords: G, C, and D. Once you have mastered playing those chords and changing from one to the other, you can use them to play countless cover songs with your band. You can even write your

If you've taken any music lessons, you'll know all about counts and bars. When you play an instrument, you play each note for a certain amount of time, measured by counts. There are different time signatures, but in the most commonly used time signature of 4/4, four counts ("one, two, three, four") make a bar. So if you play a note for "one bar," it means you hold the note for a count of four. If you play a note for "two bars," you hold it for a count of eight.

- One bar = one count of four (in 4/4 time): "One, two, three, four."
- Two bars = two counts of four, or one count of eight: "One, two, three, four. Two, two, three, four."

own songs by putting these chords in an order you like, playing them dynamically, and adding your own lyrics.

If you are not ready to start writing lyrics, you can have fun creating melodies by singing along to the music with nonsense words. There is no law that says the words or sounds you sing have to make sense! You can literally open your mouth and sing whatever comes out. You may find that by playing around with different sounds, you are able to hit a melody you like that can later be put into words. Or maybe you will find that nonsense words—or oohs and aahs—sound best in that part of the song.

Playing COVERS

HEART OF GLASS

Another way to get started is to play other people's songs, or to *cover* them. You can learn to play a song exactly as you heard it on the radio, or you can remake the song using your own style and flair. You may decide to change the way a song sounds or feels by playing it more slowly or quickly than the original recording. Either way, you can make the cover song your own by making it reflect the style of your band.

If you are interested in learning cover songs, it is a good idea to come to the first meeting prepared with your instruments and a few ideas for songs you want to play. You can buy or download sheet music for a song you like and bring copies for everyone to sight-read at rehearsal. Or, even better, e-mail the song to your bandmates a week or so in advance so that everyone has time to practice at home and can come to rehearsal more prepared. Even if everyone knows how to play the same song, there are still going to be kinks to work out, from timing and tempo to arrangement and dynamics.

TEN GREAT COVER SONGS TO PLAY

- "Cruel Summer" by Bananarama
- "Girls Just Wanna Have Fun" by Cyndi Lauper
- "Hit Me With Your Best Shot" by Pat Benatar
- "I Love Rock 'N' Roll" by Joan Jett & The Blackhearts

- "I Will Survive" by Gloria Gaynor
- "Me and Bobby McGee" by Janis Joplin
- "Queen of Hearts" by Juice Newton
- "Walking On Sunshine" by Katrina and the Waves
- "We Got The Beat" by The Go-Go's
- "You're No Good" by Linda Ronstadt

Mixing IT Up

If you are learning a song whose chord progression for the verses differs from the chorus and/or bridge, you might find it helpful to isolate certain sections and work on them individually. (See chapter 10 for more on the parts of a song.) Once you have learned how to play the verse relatively smoothly, move on to the chorus progression. Then work on putting the two parts together, paying attention to tempo, timing, and dynamics. Does the chorus have more energy, and is it louder than the verses? Should everyone play louder or should some instruments drop out of the chorus to make it more dynamic? There are countless variations you can make, and change at a later time, to drive the arrangement or order of the song. You can play around with who sings backup vocals and harmonies on different sections of the song, and create solos for various instruments throughout.

You might want to try different arrangements from one song to another so that all of your songs do not end up sounding alike. While it's good for bands to develop a particular "sound," you don't want to bore your audience with what can feel like one long endless song. Try varying speed and tempo from one song to the next, and creating a variety of moods and feelings with your songs. Of course, some bands decide to go whole hog and be all hard-core thrash sounding on every song. If that is who you are, do not let me stand in your way!

Other FUN Ways to Get Started

Here are more ideas for getting your musical vibe started:

• If there is a cover song you already know how to play, make up your own words, or change the words as you play.

• Write a song by going around in a circle—each girl writes one sentence and then folds the paper so all you can see is the last word. The next girl writes a sentence or line based on the word she can see, and so on. At the end, unfold the paper and try to sing the made-up lyrics to the tune of a song you already know.

• Any girl can start a jam session by playing something she knows on her instrument. One by one, slowly add music as each girl figures out which notes sound good with the original chords or melody. You can work up to a moment when everyone is playing and then slowly start to drop out, one by one, until the only one playing is the girl who started. Lather, rinse, and repeat, but this time have another girl start it off.

• If someone knows how to play scales, warm up together by playing and singing the notes on a scale. Start by singing the letter names of the notes, or any nonsense sounds or words you can think of. Over time, try replacing them with words or other sounds like "ah," "oh," "ooh," or a rousing chorus of "la la las." With practice, you might be able to experiment with the scales and play the notes in a different enough order for them to appear as an original melody.

coffee...tea...sushi...

FREE YOUR SONG

A Guide to Songwriting

I once heard it said that each person in the world has one hit song locked somewhere inside of them. While some people spend their whole lives trying to unleash that secret song, most people never even try. I'm not sure if the saying is true, but just imagine if it were! Think of all the unwritten songs that would be flying above our heads in the atmosphere. Maybe you will write one of those great songs. Maybe you will write many songs in the process. Maybe you are the world's next great songwriter, and all you need is some encouragement and a few ideas to help get your creative juices flowing.

Writing a song is something anyone can do—you just have to decide to do it. You might try waking up and saying, "I am going to write a song." Or, "Watch me write a song." It doesn't have to be a good song. It doesn't even have to be a song you will ever play for another living soul. It could be a practice song that you throw away or hide forever. Or it could be a song that you edit and rewrite and recycle until most of it is in the trash, but your favorite line survives and makes it into your next song, which maybe makes its way into your third album and becomes a hit . . . You never know what morsel of goodness is going to find its way into your one of your songs, and into your music.

So many things happen to us in our everyday lives, and so many thoughts and feelings can inform our songwriting. Your thoughts and feelings may be the very things other people can relate to, and that unite different people through common experiences. Music can do that. Your song can do that. Maybe it already has.

First THINGS First

There are many ways to start writing a song. It really depends on what you are comfortable with and how you get inspired. One decision is whether to start with the *lyrics* (the words) or with the music.

The lyrics can be written first in their entirety, then set to music written to fit around them. The opposite can also be done, where a piece of music is composed and then lyrics written to go with the music that match the tone, feeling, and nuances already present in the melody.

There are also a million shades of gray in between. You may prefer to start by finding a theme for what the song is about, then work on music and lyrics together. Or, you could write certain parts of the lyrics or music first and then the song can grow in any direction. Maybe you find a phrase in your journal that you feel would be a great opening line, then write music based on how those first few words make you feel. If they are mystical and magical, perhaps you will write a piano part to go with that feeling as the intro to the song. Or maybe you will find that the song begins with the chorus (as many popular songs do).

Another songwriting method is to jam and fool around with your bandmates and see what comes out. You might find that during a jam, game, or warm-up, you stumble upon a progression, melody line, lyric, or

> *I love to compose* guitar or piano parts, record them, and then start building the song instrumentally by adding bass, keyboards, and percussion. Then I start to hammer out melodies for the chorus. I usually write lyrics next and then record my chorus. The verses come easily once that's all done. —SARA QUIN, *TEGAN & SARA*

hook that you love and that could be the start of a good song. You might begin with that and then work from there to craft a song around that part, or around that lyric.

It is also possible for more than one person to contribute to a song. For example, each member of your band could write one verse, and then you could work on the chorus (or hook) together. Some songs have two hooks: a chorus and a subhook. This is great for when you have lots of ideas and find trouble deciding which part is best. Often, several parts can be used—they just need to be refined and ordered correctly. This is also a good way to bring different voices or combinations of vocal arrangements into a song.

The PARTS of a SONG

Most songs have a similar structure, but as with most creative writing projects, there is no hard and fast rule that says exactly what makes up a song. There are songs out there that have no choruses (or no verses for that matter), and one of the more outrageous songwriters out there might attempt to create a whole new song structure or arrangement that is nothing like that of the traditional song. However, there is something to be said for the more common type of song arrangements, especially when it comes to writing music that is catchy and has a chance of becoming popular or making it onto the radio. The following is a list of possible song parts and pieces that may (or may not) appear in any song you hear, in this or some other order:

INTRO • *The beginning of the song*

VERSE 1 • *There are usually three verses, but there can be more or less.*

CHORUS • *This is a "hook" that repeats throughout the song.*

VERSE 2

CHORUS

SUBHOOK (OR B PART) • *Some songs will include a second hook before or after the chorus as a lead-in or lead-out.*

VERSE 3

BRIDGE • *This is the part that brings the third verse back to the chorus.)*

CHORUS

SUBHOOK (OR B PART)

SOLOS • *Any instrument can have a solo.*

MUSICAL BREAK • *Where all instruments play together but there are no lyrics.*

OUTRO • *The ending to the song, with possible fade-out or dramatic ending.*

Here are the lyrics to "At the Party," by Northern State. The parts are marked, so you can see how it works in a real song.

CHORUS

I went to the party, It's never what it seems
I went to the party, You know what I mean?
I went to the party, Just me, a lonely MC
You can pop the cork, or you can twist the cap
I'm at this party, and I'm here to rap!

VERSE 1

I went to the party, but I couldn't get in
I asked the bouncer if he knew my girl Hesta Prynn
He said, "I know that girl, are you in that band?"
I said, "I think I'm on the list, could you stamp my hand?"

He said, "Step inside girl, you look alright
Hold up—do you satisfy the minimum height?
You gotta be this tall to ride tonight"
I said, "I might be short, but I can still party
I can shake it on the floor like Melissa Ilardi!"

VERSE 2

I went to the party, but I'll never go back,
The speakers were lousy and the jams were whack
This girl at the bar said, "Northern who?"
I said, "It's Northern State, haven't you heard of my crew?"

We rock the stage anyway we want,
I'll rock this party like a debutante
Riverdale to Gowanis
True party people want us,
Yo, keep it real, I gotta break the seal

BRIDGE

Close my eyes as I leave the house (close my eyes and I)
And then I'm at the party and I'm chillin' out (am at the party and I)
And then I'm watchin' my worries as they floatin' by (watch all my worries just)
There they go, slippin' away now (slip away)

BRIDGE, CONT'D

It's alright if you're feelin' bad (it's alright when I)
And then you're at the party and you feel so glad (am at the party
    and I)
And you wanna know if it's time to work or play (just don't know if)
Should I go or should I stay now? (I should go or stay)

PRE-CHORUS

Yo, I called you, Yo, I didn't get it
I didn't hear my cell, it didn't ring, so don't sweat it!

CHORUS

I went to the party, It's never what it seems
I went to the party, you know what I mean?
I went to the party, Just me, a lonely MC
You can pop the cork, or you can twist the cap
I'm at this party, and I'm here to rap!

VERSE 3

I went to the party, a lonely MC
All the way on Avenue D
Lookin' for Katie Cassidy
I noticed this guy was starin' at me

He said, "Hi," I said, "Hi, do I know you?"
He said, "Yeah, don't you run in that girl rap group?"
Uh huh ho, you're the one with that liberal arts college
Academic, literary kinda name, right?

I said, "Like Gorgeous George, my name is Hideous Hesta
Rhyme with pizzazz, and I am the master
Shout out to Cynthia plaster caster
Speed up the tempo and I'll go faster!"
Uh! You wanna know what it's about?
I like to party but I never go out
Mailin' and I'm maxin', callin' and I'm faxin'
I need some more relaxin', 'cause my job is real taxin'!

I got the perfect party in my mind
Y'all out on the floor, relax and unwind
And the people at the party be the NSP
No drama at the door and the drinks are free!

BRIDGE

Close my eyes as I leave the house (close my eyes and I)
And then I'm at the party and I'm chillin out (am at the party and I)
And then I'm watchin my worries as they floatin by (watch all my
    worries just)
There they go, slippin' away now (slip away)

It's alright if you're feelin bad (it's alright when I)
And then you're at the party and you feel so glad (am at the party and I)
And you wanna know if it's time to work or play (just don't know if)
Should I go or should I stay now? (I should go or stay)

PRE-CHORUS

Yo, ya know it, Yo, like Dolly said it
Workin' nine to five'll, make you crazy if you let it!

CHORUS

I went to the party, It's never what it seems
I went to the party, you know what I mean?
I went to the party, Just me, a lonely MC
You can pop the cork, or you can twist the cap
I'm at this party, And I'm here to rap!

OUTRO

In this big city, a girl can still dream
You know what I mean? You know what I mean?
Inside the hum of the big machine
You know what I mean? You know what I mean?
I feel dirty all the time and you know what I mean—
I wanna, I needa—I gotta come clean.

CHORUS

I went to the party, It's never what it seems
I went to the party, you know what I mean?
I went to the party, Just me, a lonely MC
You can pop the cork, or you can twist the cap
I'm at this party, And I'm here to rap!

Writing THE Lyrics

When writing a song, as with other forms of creative writing, there are many things to think about before you begin and as you continue the writing process. While you might set out to write one kind of song, you could find that your ideas change in midstream. You might also find that you have a lot of ideas that you are trying to fit into one song, and that your song would benefit from some structure. The following ideas are designed to help you think about what you are trying to achieve and include in your song. They are meant to help guide your thinking and writing. Not all the following ingredients need be involved in your songwriting process, but they might be helpful at some point in your songwriting career.

Voice. Who is speaking in the song? Whose perspective is it written from? Is it from the perspective of the singer and written in the first person? Or is it a story about someone else? Is it directed to the audience as a kind of warning, or is it more like a guidebook? Is it serious or silly, heartfelt or off-handed? Does it sound like it is coming from someone or somewhere else? Is it written from the perspective of an alien who just landed on this planet for the first time? Just as in a story or poem, the songwriter can play with the voice of the song to change the way the song sounds or feels.

Tempo. Is it a fast song or a slow ballad? Does it rock? Do the words go with the tempo and feeling of the song? Do you want them to? Or would you rather have the song be counterintuitive, like a slow, sweet-sounding number with lots of very fast and angry lyrics? It can go any way you want, but remember that the tempo of the piece will change the way it feels and sounds.

Tone. *Tone* describes the feeling of the words and the theme of the song. In writing, tone can refer to the feeling or mood of the words and how the words make the reader feel. Ask yourself, what is the tone of the song? Does the tone change from the verse to the chorus? Are you writing in harmony with that tone? Do you need the tone to change throughout the song to express what you are trying to say and evoke what you are trying to evoke? For example, when Northern State decided to write "At the Party," we brainstormed for everything that might fit in with the mood of a party. We also tried to write the song in a high-energy, silly manner because we didn't want to write a slow, moody song about going to a party. We wrote about being on the guest list, the sound of the music through the speakers, our friends being on the dance floor—whatever could remind the listener of what he or she might experience at a party. (See page 69-71 for all the lyrics.)

Rhyme Scheme. There are many different ways to make a song or poem rhyme. As you might recall from English class, *rhyme scheme* is the pattern of rhyming lines and is usually referred to by letters, with the same letter used for lines that rhyme. For example, with the rhyme scheme AAAA, the last word of each line rhymes. In ABAB, the last word of every other line rhymes. In AABB, the last words of the first two lines rhyme, and the last words of the last two lines rhyme.

Using a rhyme scheme can be helpful in songwriting, though having every line of a song rhyme is not crucial. You might come up with a more interesting and varied rhyme scheme, like ABCA, in which only the last word at the end of the phrase or verse rhymes with the last word in the first line. Other examples include ABCB, ABBA, AABA, and so on. Becoming familiar with different rhyme schemes will help you vary your writing and make things more interesting for the listener. Here are some examples from "At the Party," by Northern State:

AAAA

I went to the party, a lonely MC
All the way on Avenue D
Lookin' for Katie Cassidy
I noticed this guy was starin' at me

AABB

I went to the party, but I couldn't get in
I asked the bouncer if he knew my girl Hesta Prynn
He said, "I know that girl, are you in that band?"
I said, "I think I'm on the list, could you stamp my hand?"

Imagery. Imagery uses description and involves the five senses (sight, touch, hearing, taste, and smell). Imagery is using words to create a picture in your head.

These pictures can be created by figures of speech like *similes*, which compare two things using "like," "as," or "than," such as "My cat is like a furry monster." You can also use *metaphors*, which are comparisons between seemingly unrelated things using "is a," such as "The sun is a melting lollipop." Similes and metaphors can be used in songwriting to create vivid images that people can relate to and understand. You can paint a picture in your song with words and music to bring your listener into the world you are creating until they are right there with you.

Alliteration. Alliteration involves using several words in a row that begin with the same consonant sound or letter. It can sound very musical, and bring a silly sort of sound to the way we string wacky words together. The lyrics of *"Helplessly Hoping"* by Crosby, Stills and Nash are a good example. Here's the first line, "Helplessly hoping her harlequin hovers nearby."

Onomatopoeia. Some people think *Onomatopoeia* sounds like what it means: a word, or occasionally a group of words, that imitates the sound it is describing, such as "bang" or "click," or animal sounds such as "moo," "oink," "quack," or "meow." Missy Elliot wrote "Beep Beep, who's got the keys to the jeep?" Can you think of other examples?

Getting INSPIRED

Here are some techniques and ideas to help you access your inner lyricist (lyric writer).

Free Write (Or Stream of Consciousness Writing). Do you keep a journal? Have you ever found yourself writing fluidly, like there is nothing that could stop your hand from expressing the thoughts flying through your brain and the feelings pulsing through your heart? If you have, then you know how writing for yourself, with no one else to read it, can be an amazing expression of your truest, innermost thoughts and feelings.

One way to unlock the words and ideas inside you is to allow yourself to write freely—not for a school assignment or with any boundaries or limitations. Just write. Close your eyes. Let it flow. Listen to relaxing or inspiring music (without lyrics), sit somewhere peaceful (maybe outside), and allow your mind to wander. Travel to faraway places and describe what you see and how you feel. Allow your thoughts to go where your imagination takes you. Follow what happens. When the words come, don't worry about spelling, grammar, or editing. Just write. Don't stop writing. Write nonsense and make up words as you go. Write incomplete sentences or short phrases. Just write, letting the words flow from the inside out. There is no telling what you might find: poetry, a short story, a memoir, the great American novel, lyrics to the song that will change your life (or the lives of others), or simply a cute little ditty you can hum the whole way home.

Write Poetry. If you love to write poetry, you could be a natural songwriter. Many of the best songwriters are people who write poetry and then set that poetry to music. Folk music and hip-hop have many things in common with poetry, including rhyme scheme, alliteration, onomato-poeia, voice, tempo, cadence, structure, tone, and imagery. Writers like Joan Baez, Joni Mitchell, Tori Amos, and Ani DiFranco write poetically and put those words to music. Regardless of what order you do it in, you can set poetry to music or write poetic lyrics for music you or someone in your band has written.

Your lyrics can come to you anytime, anywhere. You might find yourself humming the chorus in the shower, and suddenly you've found the perfect line that was missing. If you do, sing it over and over, at least ten times, until you've rinsed all the conditioner out of your hair, and then get out of the shower and WRITE IT DOWN!!! The last thing you want to do is forget the brilliant idea you had

> **I like to write music alone, usually at night. Something happens to my brain at night when all my worries disappear and my creative side opens up. It has to do with the silence and the isolation. I set up all of my guitars and drums around me and then I'll pick up a book or turn on the TV, or do something with a low level of distraction. Pretty soon I'll find myself with a guitar in my hands and music coming out.**
>
> —KAKI KING (KAKI KING, SELF-TITLED BAND)

in the shower, or as you were falling asleep, or while you were daydreaming in biology. Keep a notebook with you *at all times:* next to the bed, in your backpack or locker, even a small one that fits in your pocket. Whenever you have an idea, scribble it down quickly before you forget. The more ideas you have, the better. There are never too many. Even if you use only a few of them, it is better to scrap things than to forget the ideas you had.

Read Old Journals. A good way to start the songwriting process is to pore over old journals and writing to mine them for ideas or phrases that standout. Even something as simple as a two-word phrase, or an interesting combination or arrangement of words (or even a list of some kind) could be the inspiration for a chorus, song title, or entire piece.

If you find something you like it, isolate it. Take it out of the journal and into the world of music. What is it you like about it? Is it the way it sounds? Is it the way certain words work together? Is there a certain way you like to pronounce the words? Can you sing them? Do you hear a melody in your head that goes with the words you chose?

◄◄ TIP ►►

Keep a list of the topics and themes on which you want to write songs in your personal lyric or band notebook. Add to it or cross items off the list as you think of things and change your mind. If you want to do this as a band, keep a wipe-off board wherever you have band meetings or rehearsals and work on the list together.

Writing THE *Music*

If you've written the lyrics first and want to start putting them to music, try reciting the lyrics aloud. Ask yourself the following questions: Are there certain stanzas or sections that stand out as particularly good? Might those sections be able to translate into a chorus if certain lines were repeated? Try reading the words at different speeds to get an idea for tempo: Does it sound better as a fast song or as a slow ballad? Can you sing any of the parts and write some kind of melody? Is there a refrain or part that should repeat? Is there a certain word or words that might be good for a song title?

But what if you are starting with music and have no idea where to begin? Try brainstorming a feeling or theme you want the song to convey. Even without lyrics, the music should express what the song is about. Is it a serious song? Is it a slow song or ballad? Is it hyper and about having fun dancing or partying? Is it an angry song with an urgent message? Even if you haven't yet decided what that message is, you can direct your playing and the notes you choose to reflect those ideas or feelings.

Once you've decided on a feeling or theme, you can start playing around. Just like the writing, rewriting, and editing of lyrics, the music can be tinkered with, changed around, and reordered. It may be helpful to think of the song as composed of different parts and then to break them down so you can concentrate on one section at a time.

A song usually begins with some kind of intro. Often a song will begin with sparse instrumentation, like a quiet piano part, a steady bass line, or a hot guitar lick. Then, after a certain number of bars, the rest of the band kicks in, or each instrument is added one at a time until the whole band is playing and the first chorus or verse begins. Other songs begin with the whole band playing, all at once, like a horse charging out of the gate. It depends on what kind of song you are writing and what effect you are going for. Maybe the drummer starts off with four clicks of her sticks, or even counting off, "One, two, three, four!" There are many ways to launch a song, and you don't have to decide immediately. You're free to change the intro, the ending, or any part that's not working at any time.

> *I prefer to write* by myself and in complete quiet. When I co-write, I enjoy writing the music and song structure/concept together and then disappearing into my own little world to write the lyrics.
>
> —ELIZABETH ELKINS, *THE SWEAR*

Finding YOUR Way

For some people it is easier to write lyrics or music in the privacy of their own surroundings, maybe in their own room, or outside in the open where one can be inspired by nature. Others like to write in groups, or on the fly. No matter what your personality or writing style, it's important to find a place and way to make up songs that feel right to you.

In my band Northern State, the three of us have very different personality types and different ways we feel most comfortable writing. For instance, I feel most comfortable writing lyrics at home on my own. I like to know roughly what we are writing about and which parts of the song need attention, but I prefer to take my assignment home to work on my parts. If some of the music has already been written, or even recorded, I take home a CD of the track, even if it is just a loop of the same chord progression or simple beat repeated over and over again, to play on my iPod—it helps get me in the mood and to realize what the song means to me. Sometimes I will take the song on a walk outside, or a jog around my neighborhood, and write down any ideas as soon as I get home. Then I usually spend another few hours just sitting quietly, listening and writing. I often use the "free write" method (discussed on page 75) to get my creative juices flowing.

On the other hand, my bandmate Hesta Prynn (aka Julie) does her best writing on the spot in the studio. She often shows up to a band meeting or recording session feeling unprepared because she hasn't written her verse, or isn't one hundred percent happy with it. Spero and I often have to remind her to relax and not get stressed out, because all of her best verses get written or finished in the studio. Once she has a chance to try out what she has written in the vocal booth, she is often able to finish her verse, or figure out a way to make what she wrote better.

For each person, the creative process can be different. Each band member has to figure out what works best for her. Trying to force someone to write something good on the spot when they are more comfortable trying things out in private is like trying to fit a square peg into a round hole. It's a waste of time, and can make creative life more frustrating than it need be.

Working WITH Your SONG

Whether you are writing a song alone or with others, the most important thing is to be open-minded and flexible. Often you won't find out until you try to play the song as a band whether different parts are working, or whether the parts are working together. Don't be afraid to scrap entire sections and try them somewhere else. One song's edits can be another song's hook. Flexibility and adaptability are crucial in songwriting. The best you can do is try different things, and make changes and edits as many times as necessary. The process can be frustrating! Sometimes the best solution is to give up on a problematic song, or just put it away for a while. Starting fresh with a new melody or theme might be the best thing if you get stuck. You can always come back to old ideas and revisit songs later, once you've gained some distance.

Songwriting can be a never-ending editing process, and often the hardest decision is when to say, "That's it! It's done!" Some bands will play the same song many different ways, or after years of playing the same song the same way, will get bored and decide to play it differently. With your own song, it is totally up to you and your bandmates how you want to perform it. You can play the same song using five different styles.

> **Something has to touch me in some way for me to tell a story about it. So the first thing is to live life. Once I have some experiences gathered up, I choose the beat and chords of the song to reflect the mood of the lyrics.**
>
> —SANDRA LILIA VELASQUEZ, *PISTOLERA*

ROCK AIN'T FREE

What Will It Cost and How to Pay For It

After being in several bands over the course of a few years since college, my bandmate and friend Katie Cassidy came up with a memorable line that was used in a song called "Rock Ain't Free." The chorus of the song repeats, "rock ain't free, but it's cheaper than therapy." It's a catchy line, and there is definitely some truth in it.

If music is important to you, and it's something you want in your life as you move through high school to college and beyond, you probably won't have an endless chorus line of anonymous benefactors. At some point, you will learn the cold, hard lesson that rock ain't free, and you can't make an omelet without breaking a few eggs. In other words, you often have to spend money on a project before you ever see a return on your investment.

The PRICE *of* FAME

Before you start rehearsing, make sure you're prepared for the costs involved. Here's a breakdown of what to expect:

Rehearsal space. If you have your own space to play in for free, such as a garage, attic, or basement, then great. If you have to rent rehearsal space, it will cost anywhere from $10 to $20 per hour, or more.

Consumables/Supplies. Beyond the cost of your instruments and gear (see chapters 6 and 8), some of the things you'll need to perform will get worn out and need to be replaced, like guitar strings and drumsticks. Guitar stings (and bass strings) need to be changed every few months and can sometimes break in midsong. Keep an extra set in your case at rehearsals and especially at a gig. You should also learn how to change a string and have the necessary tools with you to do so at all gigs, in case of an emergency. It's also a good idea to have extra guitar picks (a small flat tool shaped like a triangle, usually made of plastic, that is used to pluck or strum a guitar) on hand in case you lose them or need an extra.

Drumsticks can also break at any time and will get worn out after months of use. Keep an extra pair on hand. I play drums in Lucky Witch and sometimes, when I get really into it, I drop a stick while playing. It's wise to keep extra sticks in a special stick bag that hangs from the floor tom, just in case you need to reach in and grab a new stick without missing a beat . . . literally.

Another consumable item that all drummers should know about are *drumheads*, which are the skins of the drums that you bang on. Occasionally, if you rock too hard, you can tear through a drumhead and need to replace it. They are not too expensive and are easy to change. You will need a special tool called a *drum key*, which is used to tighten and loosen the drumhead. When you buy a drum set, or rent one at a rehearsal space, ask someone who works there to show you how to use the drum key or help you change the heads.

Other Expenses. There are plenty of other costs associated with playing in a band, from your instrument itself to other gear, to sheet music, music lessons, to transportation to and fro. (See page 88 for a list of all the things you should think about paying for.)

> **Do not go into music to make money. At first, you actually have to pay to play. Your costs will include, but are not limited to, your instruments, admission to shows (for research), clothes/costumes for playing shows, submissions to festivals, gas and food on tour, and even your sanity at times. In the end though, I think you will find it is all worth it.**
>
> —ELAINE ACOSTA, *HOT IQS*

Show ME the MONEY

You may find yourselves in the incredibly fortunate position of having parents who believe in your ability and desire to rock, and who are willing and able to pay for your music career in its entirety. Or not. Maybe your parents are proud of you, but not *that* proud, and don't feel the need or have the resources to pay for your new hobby—especially if you happen to have a new hobby every other week....

If the latter is true, there are many creative ways to pay for your new pastime—getting a job after school, babysitting, one-time events like bake sales and car washes, or even just doing extra chores.

Here are some ways to raise money for your band:

Hold a Bake Sale. Have band members bake their favorite treats and sell them after school to raise money for band expenses.

Hold a Car Wash. Set up a car wash in the school parking lot on the weekend and wash cars for five dollars each.

Organize a Craft Fair. Set up an event to sell things you and your bandmates have made, like jewelry, knitted scarves, handmade cards, or felt purses. Or learn how to make homemade paper or artworks out of interesting recycled materials.

Hold a Swap Meet. Hold an event where your bandmates and other friends swap old clothes and CDs. Charge five dollars admission to participate.

Pay Dues. You could also skip these events and go with the more straightforward plan of having each band member pay dues each week, maybe five dollars.

Keeping THINGS on TRACK

Even if your parents are initially paying for things, it is a good idea to keep tabs on your expenses. Having a band is like running a small business—learning to keep track of money spent and earned, balancing accounts, filing receipts, and recording reimbursements—these are all things we have to do as adults. What better way to learn than by trying it yourself using a band spreadsheet (see page 90) to track money spent and earned on band-related activities?

In the beginning, any money you earn should go to band members or parents who have paid for rehearsals, recording, getting merchandise printed, or other band-related costs. Keeping accurate records will help

The financial aspects **of being in a band full-time are always uncertain. The only certainty is the joy of doing what you love and the wealth of spirit you feel from it. It was scary and exciting at first, and my income was supplemented by my job as a waitress. Then we started picking up more and more gigs and our audience grew enough until we could pay our bills with the money from our shows.**

—EDIE BRICKELL, *EDIE BRICKELL & NEW BOHEMIANS*

clear up any confusion and ensure that band members are paid back so that no one feels resentful if they are spending more than others.

Once all expenses have been paid back, you might have some money left over. You'll need to decide as a band what you want to do with it. One idea is to divide it up evenly and take home the profits. Another idea— probably a wiser one—is to reinvest the money in your band. You can put it toward a recording, a line of merchandise, a website, rehearsal space, new gear, or any number of worthwhile projects. You might hold special band meetings to discuss finances and make decisions about what to do with money the band has earned, to ensure that every band member is involved in the decision-making process.

A simple spreadsheet, like the one on page 90, is helpful for bands operating on a small budget. Your band's treasurer should be in charge of tracking and organizing your band's spreadsheet and receipts. The treasurer can give a brief report at weekly or monthly meetings on how much money is in the band "account," what is still owed to people, what is need-ed to pay for rehearsals or gear, and so on. Make a photocopy of the spreadsheet printed here so you can start bookkeeping today. Income should be subtracted from expenses or vice versa to see how much money is left in the pot (or more frequently, how much more money is needed to even things out). Clearly there are more expenses than sources of income— welcome to the music business! Rock Ain't Free!!

REHEARSAL SPACE: If your band is paying for a rehearsal space, figure out your monthly costs.

MUSIC LESSONS: Include this line item if your band is trying to cover this expense. In some bands, members are responsible for covering this cost on their own.

PURCHASING OR RENTING MUSICAL INSTRUMENTS: If the band members don't all own their instruments, make sure to include this in your monthly expenses.

EQUIPMENT RENTALS: This includes monthly costs for instruments, amps, PA systems, etc.

CONSUMABLES/SUPPLIES: Monthly expenses for strings, guitar picks, drum heads, drumsticks, etc.

TRAVEL: Money spent monthly on gas, parking, tolls, bus, subway, or cab fare for getting to and back from rehearsals and gigs.

ADVERTISING: Monthly costs for running ads to look for musicians and designing and printing flyers to promote gigs.

COSTUMES: Band members may want to put money away for special clothing or accessories to wear onstage or for photo and video shoots, or the band may decide that members are responsible for paying for these items on their own.

MARKETING/PROMOTION: This money is needed to cover costs for things like a digital camera or digital video camera for photo or video shoots, making an electronic press kit (EPK), paying to host and design a band website, etc.

MERCHANDISE: In order to create merchandise for your band to sell, you'll have to lay out some money for materials. If your band starts to have an extensive merchandising operation, you may want to include this information as part of a separate budget.

RECORDING: You may want to budget some money for recording in a studio, or if recording at home, for CDs, CD cases, and other incidentals.

Ideas for Possible Sources of Monthly Income:

MONTHLY OR WEEKLY BAND DUES: Each band member contributes an agreed upon amount of money to the "pot" each week or month to help offset the band's costs and expenses.

FUND-RAISING: Bake sales, car washes, babysitting, plant watering, gutter cleaning, and leaf raking are a few ways for you and your bandmates to make money to fund your band.

GIGS: Live events where admission is charged for coming to your band's show.

CD SALES: If your band has recorded a demo, extended play (EP) or long-playing (LP) record, you can burn copies onto CDs and sell them at live shows and from your website (if you have one).

MERCHANDISE: This is the money you make from selling merch, after expenses are recouped and reimbursed to those who laid out money or supplied the raw materials.

DONATIONS/INVESTORS: It is possible that some generous benefactor will simply donate money—meaning that the parents of one of the band members might give your band money to pay for things without expecting to be reimbursed. You should keep track of this funding source as well, so you have a general idea how much money has been donated over the years. If possible, do something nice at some point to thank those people for believing in you enough to support you financially. You could make them a thank-you card; cook a nice dinner; bake cookies; buy a thank-you card, gift, or gift certificate; dedicate a song or album to your generous investors; or play a private concert just for them.

◄◄ **TIP** ►►

Keep track of your expenses by making an envelope for each category you might spend money on, such as rehearsals, gear, transportation, recording, mailings, promotional materials (flyers, posters, and so on), merchandise, and anything else. Also, create an envelope for miscellaneous expenses that do not fit into any other category. When you pay for things, put the receipt into the proper envelope. This will help you track and organize all your expenditures.

Monthly Budget for Bands Spreadsheet

Expenses	Budget	Actual
REHEARSAL SPACE	90	70
MUSIC LESSONS	130	125
PURCHASING OR RENTING MUSICAL INSTRUMENTS	30	20
EQUIPMENT RENTALS	60	40
CONSUMABLES/SUPPLIES	65	50
TRAVEL	115	100
ADVERTISING	90	80
COSTUMES	60	50
MARKETING/PROMOTION	60	55
MERCHANDISE	65	40
RECORDING	25	15
Total	780	645

Income	Budget	Actual
MONTHLY OR WEEKLY BAND DUES	40	30
FUND-RAISING	30	25
GIGS	25	20
CD SALES	50	40
MERCHANDISE	60	20
DONATIONS/INVESTORS	40	70
Total		

Net Total (Income minus expenses)	295	205

If your band becomes very successful and starts making a lot more money, it may be time to hire someone to handle your finances. A professional business manager handles the day-to-day bill paying and keeps track of all ingoing and outgoing monies. Note that before you can hire a business manager, you have to turn your band into an actual legal company, and will henceforth have to pay taxes on money you earn. Your business manager should be able to provide an accountant to do your business taxes and possibly your personal taxes, too.

My advice, gained from experience, is that no one will love your band or pay closer attention to the details of running it than you do. When things are going well for your band, it can be tempting to want to hand over certain responsibilities to managers, and business managers. The risk you run is that of losing touch with the day-to-day details of running your business. The first business management team that Northern State ever hired had difficulty opening our mail and paying our credit card bills on time. We could have kept the bills coming to one of us and handled it ourselves, but because we were on the road for a few months of the year, we were urged to have our bills sent to their office. After a few months, it became clear that our bills were not being paid on time and that our credit was suffering. It was a difficult lesson to learn, but as a small band earning a very small amount of money, our business management team was earning an even smaller percentage of that amount, making us a low priority for them to deal with.

Your band is your baby, a project you have nurtured from the first meeting with your girls, to your very first show, to the moment you find yourself paying someone to work for you. Even if your band gets so busy that you cannot keep track of all the bills and all the money you are making, you should *always* sign every check that your company writes. Do not give anyone outside your band the power to sign them for you. This will guarantee that you see with your own eyes (or one band member's eyes) where every check is going and for how much. It will help you prevent mistakes and feel secure that nothing fishy is going on when you have earned your millions!

MAKING A PLAN

Is It Time to Go Public?

We've all dreamed of being rock stars. Every one of us has stood in front of a mirror using a hairbrush as a microphone and said the words, "Thank you very much. Good night!" to imaginary crowds of screaming fans. Right? I hope it's not just me . . .

Anyway, whatever your rock 'n' roll dreams, if you're still reading this book, you have probably taken some first steps toward making those dreams come true. At this point, it might be time to make a plan to share your music with others.

How do you know when it's time to go public? Sometimes you may need a little more time for your band to grow and develop first. We'll call this stage "making a plan to make a plan," and it can go on for months (or forever). In fact, you might decide that getting together with your bandmates to play music, write songs, rehearse, have fun, eat snacks, and watch movies is THE PLAN for your band. And if that's what you decide—for now or forever—that is totally fabulous. You are choosing to make music for the love of music itself, and for the joy of creativity and self-expression. Those values should be at the core of any great band. But if you're starting to think about taking your band a step further and sharing your music with others, whether by playing a gig or recording a song, then read on.

When Northern State first decided to play in front of an audience, we started small. We were at an after-Thanksgiving dessert party at Spero's parents' house with lots of friends and family. We had written a few songs and ended up doing an impromptu performance with our friend Higbie, who is a drummer, banging on the bottom of an empty garbage can to make a beat. Our friends loved it and were talking about it so much that a friend of Hesta Prynn's heard about it and asked us to play again so he could come watch us. His band, Melomane, had a monthly residency at a small club on the Lower East Side called Luna Lounge. They were looking for an opening band for each of their shows and he wanted us to audition. We decided to throw a party at Hesta Prynn's to audition for him and invited all our friends. This time Higbie brought his djembe, an African drum, and played along with us, instead of on a garbage can!

We made an audio recording of that performance to be able to hear what we sounded like, and I will never forget the noise of the crowd laughing throughout our songs. We were definitely trying to be funny and entertaining, but there was one guy, who must have been near the tape recorder, laughing like a hyena after every punch line. We weren't sure if it was a good thing or not, but we decided to take it as a vote of confidence and a sign that we should keep writing and performing our music. Plus, Pierre offered us the gig opening for his band Melomane on a Wednesday night at Luna Lounge, and that's how we got our first official gig.

Going PUBLIC

You'll know it's time to go public once you've spent plenty of time bonding and rehearsing—that is, once you feel your band has an identity, a clear image that unites you and makes you feel like a force to be reckoned with. When you are ready to share your music and creativity with others, you'll know. But *how* to do so is a whole other question. Are you ready to play a "gig" in public? If so, where? Or would you rather start by recording a song and sharing it on your MySpace page? Chapter 14 will talk all about performing in public, and chapter 15 looks at recording a demo.

There are many ways to move your band forward, and it's important to choose the path that fits best with your band's personalities and resources. There is no single way to get from your friend's garage to the top of the charts. The only people who can decide what is best for your band are you and your bandmates. And really, no matter what you decide to do, the most important thing is to set realistic goals and to work cooperatively to achieve them.

If you've had lots of band meetings and rehearsals and still aren't sure what to do first, here are some questions to help you figure out what is right for your band:

◄◄ TIP ►►

If you could have the same career as any band in the world, which would it be? Take it from me, there is no such thing as an overnight success in the music industry. Real bands do not get "discovered" and end up playing sold-out shows at Madison Square Garden in their first year. In most cases, it takes a long time to build up your band, and there will be pitfalls and missteps along the way. Think about what lies before you on the road to becoming the band in your mind. You can set realistic goals and work toward them slowly over time.

- Do you like to perform onstage? Have you ever performed onstage before?
- Have you ever dreamed or fantasized about playing onstage in front of people?
- Do you know of a local talent show or event in which you would like to participate?
- Do you know other bands in your town that would be fun to play with?
- Is there an upcoming event or party that you think your band could be an asset to?
- Are you particularly interested in the art of recording?
- Do you have a place to record or know anyone with recording skills and/or equipment?

FIVE SIGNS YOU ARE READY TO GO PUBLIC

1. You find yourself singing songs that you wrote to your friends, or telling people about the great jam session you had at band practice the other night.
2. You turn on the radio and scan for a song you like, but nothing sounds as good to you as the song you played with your band at rehearsal.
3. You find yourself talking nonstop about your band and feel like your other friends are starting to get bored with hearing about it.
4. You cannot wait until band practice and notice that everything else in your life pales in comparison.
5. You want to share your music with friends and family, but have no way for them to see you play live or listen to your recorded music.

Our first gig was at Luna Lounge in NYC. I was terrified and really wished up until it was over that I hadn't agreed to do it. When my bandmates and I watched video of the show, I realized that I had not moved once during the entire performance—that's how terrified I was. That is definitely something I've worked on since then.

—SPERO, *NORTHERN STATE*

Keeping Your EYE on the Goal

No matter what you decide to do, having a plan—and setting short-term, realistic goals—will help you achieve it. The plan can be a bit overwhelming at first. The easiest way to avoid this feeling, and to stay on top of the plan and on the same page as your bandmates, is to set clear, concise, short-term goals every few months.

As you move forward, keep asking yourself questions like:
- What are your goals for this band? What do you want to accomplish?
- Are you getting together to play for the love of rock and to master your instruments?
- Is there a certain song you love and want to learn how to play?
- Have you written a song you want to share with others?
- Are you planning to write lots of songs and hoping to bring them to life?
- Do you have your heart set on recording an album?
- Is your dream to be part of an all-female rock band with a hit song on the radio?

Here are ten examples of short-terms goals you might decide to set:
- Play your first live show by the end of the school year.
- Make a plan to record a demo by the end of summer vacation.
- Choose which songs to record and practice them as much as possible all summer.
- Find a place to record by mid-August.
- Set the recording dates/schedule and figure out how to pay for it by September 1.
- Plan and book your second show for early fall.
- Figure out a way to burn copies of the demo to sell or give away at the show.
- Think about creating simple merchandise to sell or give away to help promote the band.
- Design a logo, posters, stickers, T-shirts, and book covers by December 1.
- Book a gig around the holidays to play and promote the band.

THE GIG

Planning for Your First Show

So you've decided to play a gig. You feel ready. Or you believe that in a few months, you could possibly be ready. In most cases, that is good enough. A musician I worked with once told me he would rather play alone in his basement for the rest of his life than get out there and make a fool of himself in front of people. My advice is the exact opposite.

Sometimes you need to get out there and play in front of people—to see how it feels, to see if you like it, and to learn what you need to do to become a better performer. I say, don't wait. Go out there and do it! Share your talent and your energy. No matter what, it will be a learning experience that will move you closer to your goals and dreams. Or, at the very least, you'll be able to look back at your first live performance someday and have a good laugh....

When the girls of Lucky Witch first got together, we weren't sure we would ever want to play our songs in public. We were playing music for the love of rock, and for our own enjoyment. After a few rehearsals it became clear that we were having too much fun not to share it with our other friends. There were six of us (plus two backup singers/dancers at our first few shows), and this made it fairly easy to plan our first show and get a lot of people to come out and see us play. If each girl invited ten people to the show, we would be playing in front of eighty people. The problem was not packing the room (a good-size club on the Lower East Side of Manhattan called Rothko), but the fact that many of us had never played our instruments in front of anyone before this gig. One thing we did to help us get ready was to hold a dress rehearsal a few nights before the gig where we invited a few of our closer friends to come hang out while we ran through the set. It was a chance for us to play in front of a small practice audience and get some feedback on how we sounded.

Even so, we were quite nervous for that first gig, and I can't say exactly how it went. Sometimes, in the excitement of a first gig, the whole experience can go by in a blur. There are a few moments where I remember messing up on the lyrics, dropping a drumstick, or making eye contact with my dad in the front row, but all in all the whole set felt like it lasted three minutes. I was a bundle of nerves and excitement. It was my first time playing the drums on a real stage, in front of a live audience. It was thrilling, as well as terrifying and awesome. And as soon as it was over, I couldn't wait to do it again.

Where WILL You PLAY?

One of the first questions you should ask is, Where will your band play?

Here are a few ideas to get you started:

- Play at a school event or party.
- Enter a battle of the bands competition.
- Enter a talent exhibition at your school or local community center.
- Play at your church, synagogue, or an outdoor location.
- Find a local club or restaurant that hosts live music.
- Hold a concert in a band member's backyard, garage, or basement.

Try researching online and in your local newspapers for events in your town, or work with school administrators to put something together at your middle school or high school. If you can't find the right event, but feel confident that your band is ready to play, find a space or venue that is appropriate and throw your own. It's best to find a space that already has sound equipment, or a hall or community center that will allow you to set up and play. Even if you haven't used a PA yet for rehearsals, you can rent a system for the performance space.

One idea is to hold your own show in a band member's or friend's garage or backyard. One big benefit of doing this is that you can set up your equipment and amps and run a dress rehearsal to hear how it all sounds in the space and what kind of gear or equipment you might need to rent so people can hear you. If you own your own PA system, it might be enough to set that up and play out of your amps and a few extra speakers. Renting gear for an event is always an option, too, but make sure you allow plenty of time to set up and create your own sound check to set levels and make sure everything can be heard before you invite an audience.

It's important to remember, however, that there might be costs associated with putting your own event together, such as renting gear. One way to raise money is to charge a "cover" at the door, or an admission price. Even if everyone pays only $5, and you have 100 people come see your band play, that's $500. It may even be enough to "make some money" to put into the band "account" for future use, or to pay back money already spent. If you decide to do this, note that you won't get the money until the day of the show, so someone will have to loan you the money in advance to pay for your gear. Or, each band member could contribute a small amount and you could raise the money together.

> *There's no feeling in* the world like having confidence in your abilities on an instrument, and getting up in front of people to share your joy.
>
> —ALICE DE BUHR, *FANNY*

Rehearsing FOR the SHOW

If you have the option, give yourselves about three months to prepare before your show. You will need a realistic rehearsal schedule leading up to the gig, with enough time to learn any new songs, and a few rehearsals long enough to "run the set" from beginning to end a few times, as the gig gets closer. It is important to practice transitions between songs so the set can be seamless, without long pauses and awkward silences. A good tip is to decide which songs you will play without any pause between them (going right from one to the other), at what point you will have a break in between songs, and who will talk to the audience and when.

Planning YOUR *Set*

A set is the list of songs you're planning to play at the show, which should be carefully organized in advance. How long are you planning on playing? Are you expected to play for a half hour? An hour? Two songs? Ten songs?

For your first show, it's best to start with a modest list, like a short set of your five best songs. Decide which songs you want to play. Pick your strongest songs that you feel could make an impact on the crowd. Are you playing any cover songs? If no one knows the music you are playing, it is a good idea to draw in the audience first with a fun cover song that everyone knows and loves.

Put the songs in the order you plan to play them, and practice them in that order. Make sure the lineup works well. Is there a part of the set that drags? Should you consider moving the slower/quieter songs around so they are not back-to-back? You don't want to bore the audience with too many slow songs following one after another. (Unless, of course, your band plays all slow songs—then I take that last comment back and apologize . . .)

◀◀ TIP ▶▶

According to Beatnik Turtle's *The Indie Band Survival Guide*, it is legal for bands to play cover songs in public venues. It is the venue's responsibility to pay music-licensing fees to the people who wrote the songs, so they get paid when bands perform their songs. Music venues usually pay one blanket fee that covers all songs played on their jukeboxes and by bands in their space.

Once you have the list of songs set in the right order, type up the list—called a *set list*—and print out a copy for each band member, plus the person doing sound. Make sure to print it out large enough so you can read it onstage (in dark lighting) from wherever you are playing. You may also want to jot down your own notes on your personal set list to help you remember chord progressions, or the first lyric in each verse, just in case you get stage fright and forget. A set list can be a sort of cheat sheet for you when you are onstage.

You should also practice making transitions from one song to the

next. You want to avoid spending a lot of time fiddling with your instruments and retuning. If you know there is a certain song where you rock out so hard you always end up out of tune at the end and need to retune before the next song, have someone with a microphone talk to the audience for a minute while everyone else retunes their instruments. You can even plan things to say during these breaks—these are known as *talking points*.

You do not have to write out exact lines for each band member to say during the show, but it is a good idea to have a loose plan of who is going to talk when, and what points you want to cover. Most important, someone should say thank you to any other bands you are playing with, to the space or venue for hosting the event, and to anyone else who helped make the gig happen. It's also good to introduce yourselves, both as a group and individually, and to thank your fans, friends, and family for coming out to support your band. If no one came to the gig, it would just be another rehearsal.

Here is an example of a set list Northern State used for a gig we played at a venue called The Annex on January 16, 2007, in New York City.

THE ANNEX 1/16/07

1. **MIC TESTER**
2. **BETTER ALREADY**—*Say hello while Katie tunes*
3. **OOOH GIRL**
4. **MOTHER MAY I?**—*Katie switches to guitar*
5. **AWAY AWAY**
6. **COLD WAR**—*Katie switches back*
7. **THE THINGS I'LL DO**
8. **AT THE PARTY**

Building YOUR FAN Base

Whenever you play live, you should pass around a clipboard with a list for people to sign up and join your mailing list. This way, you can e-mail your fans about upcoming shows, special events, or a new record, song, or piece of merchandise (known as *merch*) for sale. All you really need are first names and e-mail addresses, though if you ever plan on doing things the old-fashioned way and sending invitations in the mail, you might want to ask for mailing addresses, too. This is a great way to keep a record of potential fans for the future.

If you already have some kind of merch for sale, whether it's CDs you have recorded or T-shirts, stickers, or other band merchandise you have created, it's a good idea to tell the audience about it so they can buy some if they want. You can set up a merch table somewhere in the room and have a friend help you out by running the "booth" in exchange for getting in free on your guest list. Or you can sell the merch yourselves when you get off the stage.

Getting PEOPLE to Come to Your SHOW

Does getting one hundred people out to see your band play seem like a realistic goal? Can you make a list of one hundred people you could invite to the show? How do you plan on inviting them? Here are some ideas for spreading the word.

Use Your Mailing List. Send an e-mail to everyone on your mailing list about two weeks before a show so people can mark it down on their calendars. Then, send a reminder a day or two before the event, so they don't forget to come. Remember to include details like the address of the location, the time doors open, and what time you go onstage. If there is a cover charge or age restriction, include that information as well. Also, list any other bands that are playing, with links to their MySpace pages or websites.

Send Invitations. Create an invitation or flyer, which you can hand-deliver or mail to friends and family.

Circulate a Flyer. Create a simple flyer that you can e-mail to your friends and family. You can also print out flyers to hand out and create posters or larger flyers to hang up around your neighborhood or at your school to help promote the show.

Promote Your Show Online. Promote your gig through online communities like MySpace, blogs, and chat rooms. You may even find other bands online that are made up of girls in nearby communities or towns who you might like to invite as guests, or even to collaborate with on a gig.

Make a Guest List. If you are playing at a venue that charges a cover, the venue may allow your band to bring in a small number of guests for free. If you have rented a space and are hoping to recoup your money by charging admission, think about creating a small guest list for certain people who have helped so that you are not charging everyone to get in. You may consider putting on your guest list parents who have contributed monetarily, or close friends who have helped by making posters, promoting your show, or performing other tasks. Type up and print out your guest list, and bring it with you the night of the gig to give to whomever is working the door.

Advancing THE *Show*

About two weeks before the gig, one member of your band should call to advance the show. Advancing is done to make sure you know everything you need to know about the event, and that the people on the other end are prepared and ready for you. The first rule of advancing is that it's not always easy to get someone from a venue on the phone, and you often may need to speak to more than one person to get the answers to your questions. This is why it's a good idea to call two weeks ahead, so you have enough time to get all the information you need to make the gig run as smoothly as possible.

The second rule of advancing is that, no matter what you do, things will always be different than what you expect when you get to the gig. If they tell you to arrive at 5 p.m. to set up, do not be surprised if the doors are locked and the sound person does not arrive until 5:45. This is typical and must be expected. You have to be prepared for the worst and be flexible and calm no matter what comes your way. Advancing is a good way to try and help things run smoothly—but in this business, there is often nothing you can do to keep things from getting a little crazy. So take a deep breath, get a pen and piece of paper, and use the following advance sheet as a guideline for questions to ask when you call ahead.

Advance Sheet

LOAD-IN: What time should we arrive to set up our gear?

SOUND CHECK: What time can we check your equipment on stage?

DOORS: What time do the doors open for the event?

SHOWTIME: What time does the show begin?

ONSTAGE: What time does our band go onstage?

SET LENGTH: How long are we expected to play?

CURFEW: What time does everything need to be finished for closing?

OPENERS: What are the names of other bands that are playing before or after us, and what times do they go on?

AGE LIMITS: How old do people have to be to get in?

GUEST LIST: How many people can we can invite for free admission?

CAPACITY: How many people does the room hold?

BUYOUT: Will there be dinner provided or a buyout of some kind? (Some venues will provide a hot meal for the band, or pay a small amount of money per band member for dinner—usually $10–$15 per person.)

PARKING: Are there free parking spaces available near the location?

DRESSING ROOM: Is there a place for us to go and to keep our stuff locked safely backstage?

MERCHANDISE SPLIT: Is there a merchandise split? If so, what is the breakdown? (Some venues will let you sell merchandise like T-shirts and CDs. Most will let you keep 100% of your sales, but some will ask for a percentage. A common split is 85% for the band and 15% for the venue.)

GUARANTEE: Is there a guaranteed amount of money we are being paid?

DEPOSIT: Can you send the deposit to this address? (If you are making a guarantee, you can collect half the money up front as a deposit and then pick up the remaining half of the money on the night of the performance.)

CONTACT: Who are we supposed to speak to at the venue about our show?

PHONE NUMBERS: What is the phone number for the contact person and the venue?

ADDRESS: What is the correct address of the venue so we can get directions there and advertise the show to our fans and friends?

Advance Sheet

Date: 2019   Venue: City:

LOAD-IN:	**CAPACITY:**
SOUND CHECK:	**BUYOUT:**
DOORS:	**PARKING:**
SHOWTIME:	**DRESSING ROOM:**
ONSTAGE:	**MERCHANDISE SPLIT:**
SET LENGTH:	**GUARANTEE:**
CURFEW:	**DEPOSIT:**
OPENERS:	**CONTACT:**
AGE LIMITS:	**PHONE NUMBERS:**
GUEST LIST:	**ADDRESS:**

Be PREPARED

The purpose of something like an advance sheet—and advancing the show in general—is to help you be as informed as possible so you can deal with whatever comes your way. There is nothing you can do to ensure that things will run perfectly, but little things like coming prepared and knowing what type of gear will be available and/or what you need to bring for yourselves can help make things run better on your big night. The first gig can be fraught with obstacles and bumps in the road. Showing up prepared and with as much information as possible will help you to feel more comfortable in unfamiliar territory.

It is also a good idea to have someone with you to run interference. An older sibling who has been in a band before, or a family member or friend, can act as the band's point person. At the very least, your band should pick one person to handle all interactions with the venue or promoter. From advancing to arriving at the venue, loading in gear, setting up, checking sound, knowing at what time to take the stage, and so on—it is helpful for one person to deal with the venue rather than have each girl in the band asking lots of questions.

Down the road, you might have a tour manager do these things for you, or your own sound person to travel with you and deal with each venue as you tour. But for now, you are depending on good relations with the venue, promoter, and sound person for your night to run smoothly. Always be courteous, polite, and grateful. One thing I have learned is that you catch more flies with honey than with vinegar. Be as professional and organized as you can, while being

sweet, charming, and appreciative. The worst thing you can do is to be disorganized and come in firing millions of questions at everyone. This will set an off-key tone for the evening and can cause additional stress you definitely do not need on the night of your first gig—or any gig thereafter.

The SOUND *Check*

Once you have arrived and settled in and have been told it's okay to start loading in your gear and setting up, you will be ready for your first sound check. This means running through a small portion of your show to make sure that the sound in the venue is good and clear, balanced, and at the right volume.

The sound check can also be a cause for stress, depending on where you are playing, whether things are running on or behind schedule, whom you are working with, and what kind of gear you are using. If you are renting a PA system for the first time, and/or if the person who is helping you is inexperienced, nervous, or running late, the sound check can be especially stressful. More often than not, you will arrive at your "big gig" to find things running behind, gear malfunctioning and/or missing, and people getting on each other's nerves—and a bad sound check can make you feel even more nervous than you were already!

The best advice I can give is to be patient and organized. Have one band member be the point person for the sound engineer. When it is time to get onstage and set up your instruments, take your time to do it correctly. If you have questions, wait your turn and ask them one at time. If you can, have one band member do most of the talking and relay your questions to the sound engineer.

You will need to check one instrument at a time, making sure you have good sound on each one. The engineer will set up microphones on each piece of the drum kit (snare, kick, toms, and high hat). He or she will ask the drummer to play each part of the drum kit separately to make sure the mics are set up properly. Starting with the kick drum, the drummer should hit each part of the drum kit steadily until she is asked to move on to the next piece (usually the snare). Once the whole drum kit has been checked, it is time to move on to another instrument. The sound person will ask to hear the bass alone, and then the guitar, keyboards, vocals, and any other instruments you have in your band. While this is going on, you should all be paying attention to make sure you can hear yourselves and one another in the monitors (if you are lucky to have some kind of monitoring system onstage).

> *I really love playing* live because it's just so exciting and also scary, but the awesomest kind of scary EVER.
>
> —SOPHIE KASAKOVE, AGE 12, *CARE BEARS ON FIRE*

Finally, you will be asked to try a song all together so that the engineer can adjust the levels in the house, or audience, and onstage. It is usually best to play a whole song, giving the engineer time to get used to your sound and adjust the levels. Once you are done—again, in an organized fashion—you can ask him or her to adjust your levels onstage. You may need to hear more vocals in the monitors or less volume from the guitars, or make other refinements. Then ask if you have time to run one more song to see if the adjustments helped. If not, you can ask for a few more changes, but remember, playing in an empty room is very different from playing in one that is full of people. The sound changes because of the way sound waves are absorbed or bounce off walls and echo in an empty (more acoustically live) space. Any changes you make at the sound check might have to be altered again once you start playing the show. A good rule of thumb is to check with the crowd after the first song to make sure they can hear everyone and that the sound is okay. If not, ask the sound person, politely, to please make a few adjustments from the stage after the first song.

One thing you don't want to do is spend the whole show arguing with the sound person from the stage, asking him or her to adjust the mix in the monitors. In most cases, the audience is hearing something totally different from what you are hearing onstage, and the person doing the sound is working to make the music sound good in the PA system that the audience can hear. The monitor mix is a separate issue—only the people onstage can hear it. Although it is important to be able to hear yourselves so that you can play in time with one another and sing on key, it is more important to put on a good show and entertain the crowd. So avoid spending the whole time obsessing about tweaking the monitor mix. If you've ever seen a band play live, the last thing you want to experience is group members constantly stopping and starting between songs. You want the show to flow from one song to the next with some witty banter in between songs. As an act, you want to hold the audience's attention, and keep things interesting.

testing : testing

My favorite aspect of music is performing live, due to the interaction between the audience and the performer. There is an aliveness and a special energy when I'm in synch with people at a show that is the most wonderful feeling in the world. That is why I do music.

—PEG WOOD, *MS. LED*

LETTING YOUR STAR SHINE

Feeling Comfortable Onstage

There is no doubt about it—being in a band is not for everyone. Getting onstage and playing music you have written, or even that someone else has written, can be a nerve-wracking experience. But it can also help you break down barriers and become more comfortable with yourself. It can help you build self-confidence, self-esteem, and self-worth. Plus, not having to get up there alone can be a great relief. When you belong to a band, you are a part of something meaningful. It is much easier to get up onstage and make a fool of yourself with friends by your side than to do the same thing on your own. It can even be fun! This chapter is packed with tips on getting yourself ready, so you can have as much fun as possible once you step onto that stage.

Get IN Shape

One important way to get ready for a performance is to be well rested and in good health, so you can feel your best onstage. Getting a good night's sleep before a gig will help you stay alert and in good spirits for the show. If possible, try to sleep in an extra hour the morning of the show, or take a short "disco" nap before you get dressed and leave for the gig. Sometimes it can be hard to calm your nerves and quell your excitement enough to take a nap, but I like to tell myself I am getting my beauty rest. Even just laying in bed quietly and thinking through song lyrics or chord changes can help to calm your nerves and help you to feel more prepared for a gig.

Another good habit is eating well before a performance. Rocking requires a surprising amount of energy. I can't tell you how many times I have eaten a big dinner before a gig or even a rehearsal, only to return home afterward feeling hungry and ready to eat again. Playing the drums, especially, is a physically demanding activity that burns a ton of calories. Personally, I find that eating a meal high in carbohydrates and sugar does not provide long-term sustained energy. If I eat a piece of pizza or a bagel before playing, I most definitely get hungry during rehearsal or right after the gig. I have found that the best type of meal before a gig is a piece of lean protein (I usually eat fish), a small serving of rice or pasta, and a serving of vegetables. It's also important to always drink a lot of water to keep yourself hydrated and your voice lubricated for singing. Bring a water bottle with you to rehearsal and to a gig—you never know when you might need to wet your whistle.

And lastly, some form of moderate exercise will help keep you in shape for performances, helping you build stamina to move around onstage while singing and/or playing your instrument. Especially in a band like Northern State, with three female MCs, it is important that we can jump and dance around while we deliver our verses. It is not easy to rap when you are winded, and it is even harder to sing while you move around. I try to go for jogs, bike rides, or rollerblade a few times a week to keep my cardiovascular system in good shape. Sometimes I bring my iPod and sing or rap along to get better at breath control and to practice singing and rapping while moving around, simulating onstage behavior. I also find that consistent exercise helps me sleep better at night (so I am better rested for the gigs) and makes me feel less stressed out in general, which is always a good thing. And when I am writing lyrics, a brisk walk or jog in synch with the track on my iPod that I am writing to is a good way to generate ideas and allow my thoughts to flow freely.

Stay healthy to look and feel your best, but do not hurt yourself in any way to attain any unrealistic body type—it's not worth it. Let the music come first.
—COLLETTE MCLAFFERTY, *EDIBLERED*

What TO *Wear?*

I know. Some of you will find this section foolish. Others will wonder how I could possibly give you advice on what to wear. But all of you will one day see a picture of yourself playing with your band a few years back and think, "What on earth was I wearing???" It happens to everyone—I promise. Sometimes what seems like a good idea will appear too costumey, garish, or dressed-up later on. Or, perhaps you are going for a dressed-down look and will one day look back and wonder why you chose to wear what appears to be rags or your pajamas onstage.

Either way, the most important thing is to be comfortable onstage. You need to be able to move around and play your instrument without being hindered by some kind of unwieldy costume or ill-fitting garment. In addition to being physically comfortable, you need to feel confident and comfortable in your skin. You want to feel like you are wearing clothes—not like your clothes are wearing you. If you have to fuss with your outfit every few minutes to keep it on right, it will probably be distracting to your audience and to you. It may even detract from your performance and cause you to mess up or forget the next note or chord.

"*About fifteen minutes before* a show, I just need to go away and not speak to anyone! I stay in my 'zone' and visualize having a great show."

—COLLETTE MCLAFFERTY, *EDIBLERED*

My advice is to keep it simple. If you want to come up with some kind of coordinated look with the rest of your band, do it in a way in which everyone can be comfortable. You don't need to wear the exact same outfit to be coordinated. One thing that my side band often does is to select a few colors to work with for a particular gig. For instance, we will decide that each girl should wear whatever she wants as long as it has black, red, and white involved. Some girls will end up in mostly black with red accents, or vice versa, while others will be in black and white with no red at all. Overall the look is somewhat coordinated, and conveys the idea that we are all part of the same band, but without being too matchy-matchy. In Northern State, since there are three front women, we pick shirts to wear in bright, bold colors that look good together, like red, blue, and green. We wear the type of shirts we are each most comfortable in, with whatever we want on the bottom. But at least the three of us have brightly colored shirts on top, which help to catch the audience's eye.

Of course, some bands do go with a more coordinated, costumed look, and they pull it off incredibly well. As long as you and your bandmates are comfortable, and you all agree on what you're wearing, it can work out just fine. Just don't say I didn't warn you!

MY MOST EMBARRASSING MOMENT ONSTAGE

"One time I rushed to get to a show, and we grabbed Thai food on the way. I went onstage and was well into playing when I noticed that this girl in the front row kept staring at my shoulder. I finally looked over and there was a long Pad Thai noodle stuck to my jacket. I had to pull it off and find somewhere to put it."

—*Kaki King (Kaki King, self-titled band)*

"The most embarrassing thing that ever happened to me onstage was when my boob popped out in front of a packed house in New York City! I was wearing a silver sequined tube-top, which I later found out was supposed to be a miniskirt! What could I do?"

—*Emiko (Emiko, self-titled band)*

"When I was nine years old, I performed a saxophone solo at a recital for about three hundred people. My strap got stuck in one of the keys and kept squeaking. My music teacher had to stop the performance and fix it. I freaked out! That was my first experience with performing live. I kept trying, though!"

—*Collette McLafferty, edibleRed*

"The first time I fell down accidentally onstage was the most embarrassing. I lost my balance because I was jumping around too much. I felt like an idiot. Since then, I've done it so many times it's become part of the show."

—*Elizabeth Elkins, The Swear*

"One time my pants ripped in the butt onstage. There was a huge screen above the stage and you could see it. I remember looking up during performance and going, 'OMG, my pants are ripped!' I was mortified for a split second and then just went about my business."

—*Bianca Montalvo, Heist at Hand*

"Crying onstage. I had witnessed a terrible accident, and it really devastated me for months. In one show, I was introducing a song and for some reason ended up in tears before hundreds of people. I could hardly make it through the song—I was a mess. And as fate would have it, the show was videotaped."

—*Tracy Wilson, Dahlia Seed*

Getting READY for the Big Event

Here are some ideas to help you feel ready for your first performance:

Test Audiences. Invite a few friends to your last few rehearsals, and make one a dress rehearsal. You don't have to wear exactly what you plan to wear for the gig, but think about how you want to dress so you can feel comfortable onstage and can move around. You don't want to wear a new pair of shoes for the gig only to find out they are killing your feet, or worse, that you can't play drums in them because the heels are too high to operate the kick pedal.

Practice your music at home in front of a mirror. Think about making eye contact with your audience and trying to express how you are feeling through your music, your body language, and facial expressions. It is much more interesting to see someone onstage who is performing to the audience rather than looking down at their shoes.

Make your first performance an intimate show for a few close friends and family. Slowly work your way up to a larger audience that might include people you don't know. This way you can ease into the experience of being onstage in front of an audience.

If all else fails, imagine the audience in their underpants!

- -

Just Before the Show. Whether you are taking the stage for the first time, or are facing your two hundredth gig, it's nice to have some kind of ritual before going onstage to help calm your nerves and get you focused. The hours before a gig or show can be a hectic time, and it is easy to get overwhelmed by all the attention and/or commotion around you. If you've invited a lot of people to see your band play, or are playing at a party or event, it may seem like you are the host of your own gig, and that can feel like a lot of responsibility.

Before and after you play, you might find that a lot of time is spent schmoozing or "working the room," talking to people, thanking them for coming, and answering questions about your band. It can be emotionally draining and tire out your voice as well. It may be a good idea to find a quiet location backstage, or outside, or a separate "green room" or dressing room where you and your bandmates can get away from the crowd. Even a small audience can feel overwhelming if everyone is trying to talk to you at the same time. Make sure you save your voice for your performance and take the time to breathe deeply, drink plenty of water, go over your set list, warm up your voice, tune your instrument, or anything else that leaves you feeling calm, relaxed, focused, and ready to play.

> *I like to be* by myself, read, do jumping jacks, and change my pants
> **before a show. That's my ritual.** —SARA QUIN, *TEGAN & SARA*

It can also be a nice ritual to spend a few minutes with your bandmates before taking the stage. Northern State likes to huddle up in a circle with our arms around one another, taking a minute to thank each other for all the hard work that went into preparing for the gig and telling each other to break a leg. We usually go around in a circle, giving each person a minute or two to say a few inspirational or encouraging words. Because of the culture of our band and the nature of our personalities, someone usually takes this opportunity to make some kind of inside joke to keep the mood light. This bonding ritual has become part of what makes us feel ready to rock each night. No matter how many nights in a row we play when we are on the road, it is always nice to take a minute to look each other in the eyes and say, "Thank you. This is really fun. I'm happy we are in a band together. We are living the dream . . . "

Recording Your First Demo

Whether you have decided to make a demo first, or have played some gigs and are ready for a new challenge, this chapter will discuss different ways to record your band's music. Perhaps you think fans would like to purchase a CD or EP of your band's songs, or you want a recording to help spread the word. A demo can be used to book better gigs, get the attention of local press, get reviews, create a buzz about your band on the Internet, and sell your music to raise money for other band expenses.

This is not meant to be a complete manual that explains how each recording process works—if it were, it would already be out of date by the time you read this. Every day, new computer programs, equipment, and gear come on the scene to ease the difficulties of the recording process. More important, this chapter is meant to give you an overview of the ways you can approach the recording process, and inspire you to learn more and experiment on your own.

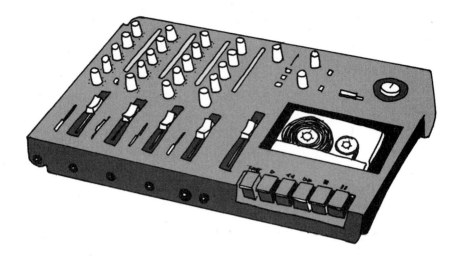

Recording ON Your OWN

There are many ways to create basic home recordings without spending too much money. I recommend doing something like this whether or not you plan to record a more professional-style demo later on.

Before any band goes into the studio to record a song or album, they usually first spend time recording home demos. In some cases, parts of the original demo make it into the final recording, because there is often no way to match the energy and raw excitement of that first recording. In other cases, early home recordings help artists learn what they want a song to sound like (or not). It can help them fine-tune the writing and structure of the song and arrangement of the instruments and vocals. And it can help the artist or producer decide how he or she wants each instrument to come across (with special effects, delays, reverb, and so on). Either way, no harm can come from experimenting with home recordings. It may be exactly what you're looking for, or it could be the first step on the road to making a more professional record.

The Four-Track. The first recording I ever made was with my bandmate Spero in her old apartment in Brooklyn with our friend Damian's four-track.

She had some idea about how to use it, but not much. We knew you could record four separate tracks at the same time, or one at a time if you wanted to, and that was about it. A *track* simply means that you can record and then listen to different parts of the music separately. For instance, the guitar can be recorded on one track and vocals on another. This way, if you mess up the words, you can go back and re-record the vocal track without having to replay the guitar part.

We plugged in two guitars and two microphones and recorded a song she wrote. I played guitar and sang backup. We recorded it in the smallest room of her apartment, basically a large closet, so we'd be away from the windows and noise outside. We sang and played the song a few times in the closet that night, rewinding and listening, and then adding and making changes. It was the most fun I'd ever had in my life up to that point.

> *When a song starts* to take shape and I hear it back for the first time through headphones, it's like magic. —SARA QUIN, *TEGAN & SARA*

Maybe you can get your hands on an old four-track recorder for cheap. You may find one lying around someone's house, or buy one used online. You could set up an overhead microphone (hanging above the drum kit) as input one, another for guitar, one for bass, and one more for vocals—and you'd be prepared for a nice little four-track recording. You'd have to experiment with mic levels, and you would have to record each track separately so as not to hear one track bleeding onto the other (if you play everything at the same time, the overhead microphone meant to record the drums would also pick up the sound of the guitar, bass, and vocals). But although it involves much practice, it is a fun way to play around in your rehearsal space and get an idea of what you sound like as a band. This is helpful not only in the recording process, but also in the rehearsal process. Sometimes, hearing a recording of a song will help you realize the arrangement isn't working, or that something needs to be played differently (faster, slower, more in tune, whatever . . .).

Making a Live Recording. Another option is to record your band playing live. One way to do that is to ask someone at the venue where you're playing if they can create a *soundboard recording* for you. If someone in your band has a digital recording device, you can plug it into the soundboard and get a mix that sounds exactly like what's coming out of the speakers at your show. The venue might already have this kind of setup, and it might be easy for them to burn you a CD of the show.

You can also do this by plugging a special microphone into an iPod or MP3 player. Someone in the crowd can hold your iPod and get a recording of what your band sounds like live in the room. You can also record rehearsals that way, or even separate tracks of your songs (vocals, guitar, bass) and then import those recorded tracks into your computer to play with GarageBand or another digital audio program.

Using GarageBand. All Macintosh computers now come with a built-in microphone and a program called GarageBand. It is relatively easy to use (you can always go to the Mac website to learn more or get help), and with it you can record anything the microphone picks up. You can create as many tracks as you want, allowing you to record drums, bass, guitars, vocals, and any other instrument separately.

The beauty of Garage-Band is that once things are recorded, you can see each instrument as a digital file and can copy, paste, edit, and move things around. If the bass line was played perfectly during the intro but then went astray, you can copy and paste the first four bars of the bass line throughout the rest of the tracks. If you want to add a break where everything drops out except the bass and drums, you can do that by muting the guitars and whatever sound remains for a certain section. You have the freedom to play with each track separately, moving them around, adding effects, making sounds louder or quieter, fixing mistakes, or simply enhancing what you have.

GarageBand is constantly being updated; by the time you read this there will probably be even more things you can do with it. Or perhaps Mac has even replaced GarageBand with something new and better! The point is, there are relatively simple computer programs out there that are affordable and easy to use. It's best simply to get one and play with it. Try making a test recording, even if it's just you singing into your computer while strumming an acoustic guitar. Experiment with the recording process. See what it's like to manipulate audio and add vocal effects. Learn about what you like and don't like. This will help prepare you for whatever recording you do in the future. If you find yourself lucky enough to record in a studio, with a professional producer and/or engineer, any experience you have gained will help you ask informed questions and make you an educated artist.

Using Pro Tools. Most professional recording studios use a Pro Tools (by Digidesign) setup. Pro Tools is a digital audio workstation. It works similarly to GarageBand but is more sophisticated and complex.

Pro Tools is integrated with audio gear in a studio to allow for each instrument to be recorded separately—not just into one microphone built into a computer, but as if the computer itself had as many inputs as you wanted to use (like a four-track, but with unlimited tracks). Instruments can be recorded on separate tracks and then manipulated digitally. It can also be used to create beats and loops using electronic drums, basses, guitars, and any other instrument—all using the program itself, without any physical instruments in the room.

A professional Pro Tools setup is expensive and requires a specially designed computer and a host of other equipment. But you might find someone with a smaller, more portable Pro Tools rig called Pro Tools LE, also made by Digidesign. Pro Tools LE is for people interested in making recordings that sound more professional and who can afford some gear, but who don't have the space or desire to create an entire recording studio. With LE, all you need is a computer to run the program and either an MBox or a Digi 002. The MBox gets connected to the computer and has two input channels; the Digi 002 has several inputs.

If you know someone with a Pro Tools LE setup who is looking to learn more about the recording process or get experience as a sound engineer or producer, ask if he or she is willing to set up and record your band for a small fee, or for the opportunity to be the producer or engineer on your record. The convenient part is that it is a relatively portable setup and can be moved anywhere. With Pro Tools LE, there are a limited number of inputs that can be used at the same time, but someone who knows how to use it should be able to record whatever you want, do basic edits, and add any effects.

I encourage women to educate themselves as much as they can about how a live sound system or recording studio works. It is very empowering when you know enough about what you're talking about to have people take you seriously and be wise to all the aspects of making music.

—KAKI KING *(KAKI KING, SELF-TITLED BAND)*

Studio RECORDING

The options mentioned above are all great ways to experiment with recording. If, after all that, you still don't have a decent demo, or you are ready to record a full-length album (LP) or a shorter album (EP) to sell to your fans and need a professional-sounding recording, it might be time to find a local recording studio.

Finding a Studio. Audio engineers and producers spend years learning how to use Pro Tools, working in studios, and slowly building their own studios. If you happen to know someone who owns a studio, or works at one, he or she may be willing to help you record a demo for free, or for a small fee (you will probably need to pay to rent the studio space). Or, you may be able to hire someone to produce your record "on spec," which means you would not have to pay them up front, but only if and when you make money selling copies of your record. This can get complicated and might even require a legal agreement, which needs to be written (or at least approved) by a lawyer, and can cost money. For your first recording, it is best to find someone who will do it for you as a favor, or a place where you can pay an hourly fee up front to record, and not owe any money "on the back end."

The *audio engineer* is the person who sits behind "the boards" and actually records your band. In some studios, the producer does the engineering, or recording, but usually the producer works with an engineer. The engineer does not usually offer his or her opinion about the recording but focuses on setting up microphones, checking levels, and recording and editing takes. In most cases, the producer and engineer work in one room and the recording takes place in a separate room or booth (called the *live room* or *vocal booth*). Once you are inside the live room or vocal

> **There will always be** people who will try to discourage you. Don't listen to them! Don't work with ANYONE who has a sexist or negative view of female musicians. Surround yourself only with positive, can-do people.
>
> —COLLETTE MCLAFFERTY, *EDIBLERED*

booth, you have to wear headphones (called *cans*) and speak into a microphone to communicate with the engineer and producer. They can speak back to you through your cans when they press the talkback button on the mixing board.

The producer is usually hired to help a band realize how they want their recording to sound. A producer can be involved on many levels, from the actual writing and arranging to suggesting effects and equipment to get different sounds out of different instruments. It is up to you and your band to decide how involved you would like the producer to be. It is also possible to produce your own record and hire an audio engineer to do the recording. Another option is to co-produce your record with a producer who has more experience and whom you trust.

Pre-Production. Once you find a studio and know who you will be working with, how much it will cost, and how much time you will have, it's a good idea to make plans for *pre-production.* The more time you spend writing and rehearsing before you go into the studio, the more prepared you will be for the recording process. Things can always change once you are in the studio, and it is best to be open-minded about song and vocal arrangements, new ideas for choruses and hooks, sound effects, and other production ideas that band members, producers, and engineers might bring to the session. However, you should be able to play the songs you plan to record backwards and forwards, and have an idea of how you want the recording to sound. You should go in feeling confident of your ability to express opinions and direct the recording session to your specifications.

The Pressures of Studio Recording. No matter who you work with in the studio, it is important that you feel comfortable expressing your opinions and standing up for what you believe works in your own music. The worst feeling is to pay all sorts of money to record a song (or a few songs) but believe it didn't come out the way you wanted because the producer or engineer did not pay enough attention to your ideas.

Always meet with whomever you plan to work with *before* you enter the studio in order to discuss your thoughts and make sure there is open and honest communication. If you find that it is not a great match, keep looking for someone else who better understands your project. The most important thing is to feel empowered to make the decisions you want. If you want the intro to be a cappella, you can have the intro be a cappella! Do not allow yourself to be bullied into a guitar solo intro that you don't like and don't want to play. On the other hand, it's also important to stay open-minded about trying new things and experimenting with your sound. It's a tough balance, but certainly worth it, as you never know what someone else's perspective might do to improve the sound of your band. Your recording should sound like *your* band, but also be unique and interesting enough to stand out among the millions of bands recording demos every day.

In some cases, producers or engineers might suggest having studio musicians, or even the producers or engineers themselves, play an instrumental part in the recording. This is quite common, and might be very helpful. Again, just make sure you are a part of the decision-making process. What you want to prevent is having a band member play a certain part and then for an engineer or producer to re-record that part without telling you, or telling you after the fact. All communication should be done up front and out in the open. This way you can decide together—as a band—whether you are happy with the way things sound. If not, and the producers and/or engineers have an idea to help improve the recording, you can try their suggestion and see if it helps.

Your first recording experience should be empowering, and in a nurturing environment where you are encouraged to experiment. You need to be allowed to make mistakes. There are simple ways to edit out mistakes or redo isolated sections until you get them right. If you are using Pro Tools, or some other digital recording interface, you can literally "punch in" isolated sections to redo them, without playing the whole song all over again. If one or two notes, or a small section, gets messed up, it is very easy for an engineer to re-record that small section without compromising the rest of the take.

In most cases, you will record each song (or each verse or chorus) a few times, after which the engineer and producer will "comp," or compile, the takes so you have the best possible sound on every note. You can be a part of the process of listening back to different takes and pointing out which parts you like and why. If you like the first note of one take, the last note of another, and the middle section of a third, a skilled engineer can paste those pieces together seamlessly so the listener cannot tell they came from different takes. When you are listening, look not only for the correct notes and singing on key, but also for the highest energy, the moodiest feeling, or whatever you are shooting for in that particular song. Obviously, some engineers are more skilled than others—in some cases, it might be quicker to just re-record a section than to make the edits. Be sensitive to the people you are working with, and work together to achieve the best possible recording with the fewest possible headaches.

The studio is a place to experiment a bit, without wasting too much time. Maybe, for example, you have always played a certain song in a dark, moody, quiet way, but after recording it and listening back, you find it sounds even better louder and faster and with more of a rock feeling. Or, you might find that to achieve the dark, moody emotion, you have to play it even quieter and more slowly in the studio—or add a creepy keyboard sound that you don't normally employ live. Experimenting like this can be a lot of fun and will help solidify the bond between you and your bandmates.

It can also be mentally exhausting. After hours of playing, recording, and listening back (especially over headphones, or cans), your ears may feel fatigue, and you can get too tired to make decisions. When and if this happens, take a break and walk around outside. After a while it can become difficult to hear the differences between takes. Sometimes, you need to call it quits and come back the next day with fresh ears, so you can listen with an open mind and make decisions about what you have recorded.

- -

Mixing and Mastering. Most likely, the same engineer who records your demo will do the mixing and mastering. *Mixing* is the process during which the levels (volume, frequency, and dynamics) are set for the various instrumental parts and vocals you recorded. You can make certain parts louder or softer; add echo, reverb, or other effects; and even "pan" different sounds from one speaker to the other (so the sound actually moves across the room, or from one ear to the other if you listen with headphones). In more professional recording situations (and for more money), separate engineers can be hired who specialize in mixing. Sometimes artists leave the mixing process to the engineers, but usually artists like to be involved and present at mixing sessions, making sure the mix is to their liking and they can hear everything they desire in the recording.

The same can be said for the mastering process. Mastering is the preparatory stage after which the mixed recording can be made into digital files for CDs or MP3s. In some cases, separate masters must be made to prepare a recording for vinyl records. For your purposes, the engineer who recorded and mixed your demo will probably use a digital program to master the recording so that it is ready to be "bounced" and "burned" as a CD, or e-mailed around as an MP3 or other digital music file. In more professional recording, a separate mastering engineer is hired. There are people who master records full time, working in mastering facilities as the final set of ears on every record they work on.

Mastering is an exciting part of the process: the final step of recording. You must come prepared for the mastering session, knowing in which order you want the songs to appear on your demo or record. The mastering process also ensures that sound levels are even from one song to the next, so the listener does not have to adjust the volume when listening to your record.

PRODUCING *and* DISTRIBUTING *Your Demo*

Once you have a mastered copy of your record or demo, you are ready to burn CDs to sell at your shows or pass around to spread the word about your band. You can also upload MP3s onto your band's MySpace page or website, and/or e-mail MP3s to everyone on your mailing list. There are many ways to distribute your music digitally. You might also be interested in paying a company to manufacture and produce a large quantity of CDs. If you do, you will need to supply the original master and some kind of artwork for the cover, back cover, and disk label itself.

There is also something in the music industry called a P&D (production and distribution) deal. This is when you pay a company not only to manufacture and produce copies of your record, but also to distribute the copies to specialty record stores. Unless you plan to tour the country promoting your release, it doesn't make much sense to invest in a P&D deal. But if you are serious about a career in the music industry someday, it's good to understand how that works. If you were ever to sign a deal with a label or record company, they would pay to manufacture and distribute your record in stores all over the country.

ALMOST FAMOUS

How to Spread the Word

If you're dreaming of becoming a famous rock star, I'm here to tell you that there is only one way to do it. And it doesn't happen overnight. The only way to spread your music is to do it yourself, from the very beginning. This includes practicing, getting experience, playing, learning, and growing, but also means building on a group of supportive fans you meet and impress along the way, one person at a time.

The more people you can get interested in the music you are making, the easier it will be to find places to play and sell records and merch. You begin with your immediate friends and family and watch as they spread the word to their friends and other people at school. As more people hear about your band, it is up to you to practice and make sure you work hard to learn new songs, sound good, and improve your live show. If you succeed, more and more people will want to come see you play each time.

Using THE Internet

In today's world, there are so many ways to promote your band and create a community of fans online. I often wonder how any bands before 1995 ever got anything accomplished! When I was in middle school and then in high school, my older brother had a band called The Sunshine Spider. Every time they wanted to let their fans know about a show, they had to print postcards announcing the show and physically mail them out to everyone on their mailing list. It was expensive and took up a lot of time. These days, most music industry communication is conducted over e-mail and through band websites, online communities like MySpace, and via the blogging world. It is never too early to create a home for your band on the Internet.

Joining Online Communities. On websites like MySpace, your band can network, create a community of friends, build up a digital mailing list to share your music and promote your upcoming shows, as well as upload band pictures, graphics, music, and information about your band so people who are browsing might find you. It's easy (and free) to create a MySpace page, and there are many other websites to choose from, such as Pure Volume and Facebook.

One of the main benefits of having an online community is the ability to network and get acquainted with other female musicians in your community or neighboring towns. You might find other musicians to play with, or other bands of young women to team up with for events or shows. It's a great way to become friends with other artists and make amazing things happen!

◀◀ TIP ▶▶

The Internet is a great place to network, make friends, and expand your fan base, but it can also be a dangerous place if you're not careful. Whether you are on MySpace or any other networking website, remember to be safe and smart at all times. Be on the lookout for signs of trouble, and always let your parents be involved. Never give out personal information (phone number, address, or last name) over the Internet or make plans to meet someone alone, in person, that you met online. It's important to remember that not everyone you meet online is who they say there are. If someone suggests you meet him or her in private because he loves your music and wants to help your career, be wary and tell your parents about the interaction. It could be someone much older than they say they are, posing as a young musician or music industry person. If a real relationship is going to develop with a friend online, it will happen slowly and naturally over time. You can meet up with other bands or musicians at a supervised gig or rehearsal space.

Creating Your Own Website. You can also create a website for your band. You will have to pay to host the site and for your domain name, but these things are not very expensive, and if your band is playing gigs, you might be able to use the money you make to reimburse whomever is paying those costs.

You will need someone with graphic design and web programming skills to help set up your site, but these days it is pretty easy to create and maintain a simple web site. Is there a girl in your band who already knows how to design and program a website? Or someone in your class who is great at computer stuff and wants to get involved with your band? Giving him or her the job of being the band's graphic designer is a great way to expand your inner circle (or posse) and get more people onboard. If the band's graphic designer is invested in seeing his or her artwork spread around the Internet and your town, she will likely be more eager to help make those things happen. Here are a few things to post on your band's website:

BIOS. One page of your website should be a brief "bio" of your band, explaining who you are and how you got started. Your bio should be written in a friendly, interesting fashion—you don't want it to be too dry and boring. Look around at some websites and MySpace pages of bands you love and read their bios. See if they inspire you. Most bands write their bio in the third person, meaning that it is written from the perspective of someone who is not in the band. You might try doing it differently and experimenting with the perspective and voice. You want it to read the way your band sounds. When people go to your website to learn about your group, they should get more than just the facts. They should get a sense of what you are about from the look and feel of the site and how you have chosen to represent yourselves.

◀◀ TIP ▶▶

If someone creates a logo for your band, it is very important to always give credit. Allow the artist to write his or her name in very small letters in the bottom corner of the logo, so people will know who designed it. You might also have a page on your website listing people you want to thank, including artists and designers who have helped you, with links to their websites or MySpace pages. You should also offer guest list spots to people who have helped your band for no charge, so they do not have to pay to see you play.

PHOTOS. One way to give the world a taste of your band is by supplying a page of photos. Include pictures of your band playing live, or rehearsing. You might want to include candid shots of your band hanging out and doing funny or more "regular" things, as well as more posed "glamour style" shots. Here is where having someone in your band or a close friend who likes to take photographs comes in handy. Anyone with a digital camera can take pictures and e-mail them around, after which you can upload the pics onto your website or MySpace page. Always list photographers' names with the pictures, giving them credit for their work.

. . . .

MAILING LIST. Another page on your site should be dedicated to your mailing list. You should have a place where fans and friends can sign up to join your list. Ideally, someone can set it up so that all names included on the list are automatically added to a database or file of names. If not, you can set it up so that every time someone signs up, an e-mail gets sent to one band member with the new person's name and e-mail address; that person then has the job of maintaining and updating the mailing list.

. . . .

MUSIC. If you have recorded a demo or a live show, you can have a music page with tracks uploaded for your fans. You'll have to decide whether you want the songs to be in "downloadable" format (meaning that you are giving them away) or "streaming" (people can listen to them on your website, but not download them).

Another thing to decide is whether you want to stream a whole song or just parts of it so that you give people a taste without giving away the whole song. This has to do with your philosophy about the music industry and what you plan to do with your music. If you are trying to sell copies of your record, you might not want to give your music away. However, giving away your music in the beginning is a great way to spread the word about your band, so people can hear the music you have recorded. If you have a few tracks available for free download, it might get people's attention. People might end up passing your music around, or writing about it on their blogs. It could help your band get bigger and better gigs, attract more of an audience, a larger mailing list, and a general fan base so that once you record an album, more people will want to buy it.

The music industry is constantly in flux and there is no definitive answer to this question. I would say that in the beginning of your musical career, no harm can come from giving away a few songs to help build your fan base. At some point, if you invest in the recording of an album, selling copies of the CD or MP3s on iTunes or other similar sites may be a good way to earn that money back.

. . . .

MERCHANDISE. If you have created merchandise with your band's logo or graphics (see below), include a merchandise page on your site where fans can purchase it. You can do this fairly simply by setting up a PayPal account and linking it to your website, but you will most definitely need a parent's permission and help to link it to some kind of bank account or credit card.

. . . .

MORE IDEAS. Here are more things you might put on your site:
- A page with news and updates about the band.
- A blog.
- A message board where fans can write messages to your band and to one another.
- A contact page with your e-mail addresses and a contact person if someone wants to book your band for a show or event, write an article about your band, or do an interview.
- A place to list upcoming shows and events.
- A press page with links to any articles written about your band, or scanned-in copies of articles and listings in local papers.

Blogging. In addition to having a MySpace page and your own website, it is a good idea to get involved with the online blogging community. You can read and write about other bands and spread the word about your own band, especially if you have an upcoming show, event, or record. Blogs are a great way to reach out to the music community and learn about other bands you might like to play with or open for (or have open for you), and a chance to meet people who might buy your record or write about your band.

> *Even though we are* signed with a label, we still do a lot of booking, publicity, accounting...the business side is almost my nine-to-five job. I do hours of e-mails and phone calls every day!
>
> —COLLETTE MCLAFFERTY, *EDIBLERED*

Promoting YOURSELF the OLD-FASHIONED Way

Whether you have a strong online presence or not, there is nothing wrong with doing things the old-fashioned way as well. Creating simple posters, flyers, and invitations for your gigs that you can hang up and hand out at school and around town will most definitely be a helpful reminder to your friends and potential new fans that your band exists and that you are playing an upcoming gig. Often, it is easier for people to remember an event if they have an actual physical invitation to hold in their hands—something they can fold up, put in their back pocket, and find later on, slightly shredded after it's been through the wash. Not to mention the personal touch of printing out postcards to advertise your show and then writing personal notes to people on the back, inviting them to attend and expressing how important it is to you that they be there.

If you are designing a poster or flyer using a computer program like Photoshop, it's always a good idea to save it as a JPEG file. This way you can e-mail it around to your mailing list or upload it onto MySpace or your band's website to use as an online invitation. Remember that if you plan to print out flyers and posters there will be costs associated with paper and ink (if you are printing at home) or having it printed at a place like FedEx Kinko's, or Staples. A good way to save money on printing costs is to design a one-color image and to print it on a light-colored paper, rather than paying for a full-color layout.

The best way to promote is hand-to-hand combat. MySpace has definitely revolutionized music promotion and it has enabled bands to reach fans all over the world. However, putting up posters and handing out fliers is the best way to get to know your fans and potential fans, and for them to get acquainted with you, in your hometown. —ELAINE ACOSTA, *HOT IQS*

There are also companies that will print higher-quality flyers and posters (usually on slightly thicker card stock) that you can order online by uploading your artwork. This is more expensive than printing a few flyers or posters yourself, and usually involves a minimum order of a few hundred pieces, but could be considered at some point in your band's career as an investment in a really important gig that you want to promote more professionally. To place orders online you will most likely need a credit card and therefore a parent's permission and willingness to help by laying out the money to be reimbursed when the band earns it back.

Another great way to help promote your band is to get your event listed in local papers and entertainment magazines. The best way to do this is usually to send an e-mail to the person who handles listings at each publication. It does not cost you anything to be included in listings, and it is a great way to advertise without spending money. Another amazing form of promotion is the local press. If you can get someone who works at a paper or magazine interested in your band, your band's message, or an event your band is putting together (maybe it's a charity to help raise money for a great cause), you might be able to get a write-up, interview, or article about you into the paper or some alternative publication. Not only will many new people read and learn about your band for the first time, but it will also be very exciting to see your name (and possibly your faces) in print!

Making DIY Merchandise

There is a wide range of merchandise you can create that will sport your band's logo or graphics—from T-shirts to stickers, buttons, coffee mugs, key chains, yo-yos, and more. There are lots of ways to make low-price merchandise, which you can sell to your fans and friends to make back the cost of the things you bought. Here are just a few ideas for quick-and-easy items:

- Buy T-shirt transfer paper, available at crafts and office supply stores. Get an image of your band, whether a photo or your logo, and follow the instructions to put the image on T-shirts, backpacks, or other accessories.
- There are tons of websites where you can order stickers, stamps, buttons, and many other things to be printed with your band logo.
- Making book covers for your textbooks can be done by making a stencil of your band logo and then painting or drawing it onto paper you cut into book cover–size pieces.

Producing a MUSIC Video

Especially with online video websites like YouTube, a relatively unknown band's music video can catch on like wildfire and propel a band into stardom. And because the quality of video on YouTube is so low anyway, the video itself can be very low budget.

Spend some time on YouTube watching videos of some of your favorite bands. Think of a funny or interesting idea for a video that you can shoot on your own or with the help of a friend and a digital video camera. Shooting outside tends to be better for lighting—you might have to experiment a bit before you are happy with a location and concept. You can shoot the video in one take from start to finish, or film a whole bunch of footage and edit it together using a program like iMovie, which you'll find on your Mac.

You can pay people to film and/or edit your music video professionally (or semi-professionally), but in the early stages of your career, making a low-cost video with your friends and editing it with a program like iMovie can be a fun-filled learning experience, and in the end you will have a great promotional tool for your band. Upload the video onto your band's MySpace page, wesbite, YouTube—wherever you want. If you hire a professional, you risk spending a lot of money for something you may or may not like. Doing it yourself will guarantee that you are proud of the outcome, even if it is sloppy and imperfect. Here are some possible ideas for your music video:

- Film yourselves at a nearby amusement park riding roller coasters and other scary rides, waiting on line, and eating cotton candy and candy apples.
- Film yourselves shopping at the mall and hanging out on benches, making wishes in the fountain, and playing games at the arcade.
- Film yourselves playing miniature golf, posing near the small-scale architecture.
- Film yourselves bowling, putting on the funny shoes and hanging out together in the bowling alley.
- Film yourselves down by the waterfront, on the boardwalk, eating beach food and playing in the sand.
- Film yourselves on a playground you used to go to when you were little. Ride the swings and hang upside down from the monkey bars.
- Film yourselves on the school bus, sitting three in a seat, carrying your instruments, doing some last-minute studying, doodling, or daydreaming out the window.
- Film yourselves at recess or after school playing an organized game like kickball.
- Film yourselves all dressed up like a glamour band pretending to perform your song.
- Film yourselves dressed up like boys pretending to be a band performing your song.

WHEN THE GOING GETS TOUGH

Dealing with Drama Queens, Disagreements, and Temptations Along the Way

Lots of bands end in the same way—with big fights, "creative differences," and bandmates hating each other and no longer on speaking terms. If you do not want your band to fizzle out like this, you have to work hard every day at keeping communication alive. It is no easy task.

You have come together over a love of music, but that is a broad topic with lots of variables. There are many things to argue and disagree about, and decisions need to be made on every level, almost every day. What songs should you play, and how should you play them? Who will perform (and sing) which parts? Who should be louder (and who quieter)? Where and when you should play? Who should you play with? When is it time to record? At that juncture, which songs will you record, and when, where, how, and with whom?

Questions like these can go forever, each creating opportunities for band-mates to argue and fight. Read on for tips on keeping your girls together when the going gets tough, and for working out the differences among yourselves.

From day one, it has not been easy. We have disagreed, argued, fought, not spoken, made up, been the best of friends, been the worst of enemies, and at times inspired, resented, learned from, been there for, connected with, and disappointed one another. We've experienced the highest of highs: our first gig, first interview, first great review, first recording session, first fan mail, first autograph, first recording, first television appearance, radio appearance, photo shoot, tour around the country, and then the world. We've opened for bands we have loved and admired since we were little girls. We have signed a record contract with a major label. We made a record with producers we respected. We stayed in fancy hotels and ordered room service by the pool. We have also shared the lowest of lows: the disappointment of not selling more records, leaving our major label, parting ways with people we loved working with because we could no longer pay them, and wondering if we made the right choices.

◀◀ TIP ▶▶

Your band should feel like a group of girls with one strong voice and a clear message or purpose. This will hopefully develop over time, through your experiences together. Scheduling fun band activities outside of or in addition to rehearsals is one way to help foster this feeling of camaraderie.

We have picked up the pieces and gotten back on our horse after falling off. We returned to the studio to write new songs, experiment musically, and inspire one another again.

At times, being in a band can feel like a roller-coaster ride, but remember that you have chosen to get on it with your bandmates, who are your friends and your girls. Do yourselves a favor and be patient with one another. Listen more until the moment comes to speak. Think about other people's ideas and take time to mull things over before you react. Keep the lines of communication open. Be as honest and forthright as you can without being bossy and pushy. Be who you are and express yourself creatively, but don't stifle the creativity of those around you. Try to let the creative process flow through you. Let one another's ideas bounce around the room and take shape, and be a good facilitator of other people's ideas. If that is not your strength, let someone else take on that role. Be open, loving, kind, and respectful. Do

Dealing with Drama Queens, Disagreements, and Temptations Along the Way

Lots of bands end in the same way—with big fights, "creative differences," and bandmates hating each other and no longer on speaking terms. If you do not want your band to fizzle out like this, you have to work hard every day at keeping communication alive. It is no easy task.

You have come together over a love of music, but that is a broad topic with lots of variables. There are many things to argue and disagree about, and decisions need to be made on every level, almost every day. What songs should you play, and how should you play them? Who will perform (and sing) which parts? Who should be louder (and who quieter)? Where and when you should play? Who should you play with? When is it time to record? At that juncture, which songs will you record, and when, where, how, and with whom?

Questions like these can go forever, each creating opportunities for band-mates to argue and fight. Read on for tips on keeping your girls together when the going gets tough, and for working out the differences among yourselves.

In the HEAT of the MOMENT

The dynamics of your band have a lot to do with the different personalities you are bringing together. Each member brings a rich array of talent, ideas, and versatility into the mix. These gifts are what will make your band interesting and compelling, but they are also what can make being in a band challenging. There are *definitely* going to be differences of opinion, and times when tempers flare. How you deal with these conflicts will shape not only your relationships with your bandmates, but the experience of everyone concerned. If you're not having fun, you can be sure your audience isn't either.

There are many ways to deal with disagreements in the heat of the moment. One band member might be particularly good at helping others to hear each other out and hash out a compromise. Or, you might find that two girls have a particularly heated vibe and need to go through the motions of disagreeing before they can compromise or see eye to eye. Sometimes, the best solution is agreeing to disagree in the moment, then letting everyone take the problem home to think about and discuss later. A little distance from a heated debate can help people rethink their position and try to see things from other people's perspectives.

As with any set of relationships, being a member of a band is not easy. But even though there are hard times, the reward of making it through the rough patches is working together as a team to create music everyone can be proud of.

NEVER try to resolve conflicts when you're upset. Wait till everyone's cooled off and can think logically again. Whatever happens, your friendship is the most important thing. —BIANCA MONTALVO, *HEIST AT HAND*

Dealing WITH Differences

It is crucial that you find a way to deal with band questions that gives each member an active voice in the decision-making process. As mentioned before, a weekly meeting (in addition to rehearsals) is a great way to discuss business and allow each girl to express her opinions and ideas. Setting time aside to talk things through is a great way to start, but that doesn't always solve the problem of differences of opinion and potentially bruised egos.

Some of the very same people whose creative, outgoing personalities inspire their dreams of being rock stars and playing in a band can also have the reputation of being self-centered and difficult. Perhaps you know someone with a personality like that? Maybe there is someone is your band who is difficult to communicate with, isn't a good listener, or doesn't like to compromise? Maybe that person is you, or your best friend. Or both.

It's likely that if you have a band consisting of several people, at least one of them will have some "difficult" personality trait. There is almost no way around it. In fact, if there is only one in the group, you should consider yourself lucky. But if you want your band to be successful and productive, you have to work through your differences and use them to your advantage. Often, the very same person who is difficult to work with also brings a lot to the group dynamic. There is good and bad in every person, and if you are committed to working together, you have to figure out a way to deal with one another's quirks and hang-ups.

We have learned that communication is key. To avoid miscommunication, we send daily e-mails to keep the band in the loop. If there is a conflict, we sit down and talk about it. Listening is key.

—COLLETTE MCLAFFERTY, *EDIBLERED*

In some cases, allowing extra time to make difficult decisions will be a great help. If you know that band members feel strongly about certain topics (like how a specific song should be recorded), allow time for that discussion *before* you go into the studio to record, especially if you are paying for studio time. You don't want to find yourself in a situation where you are paying someone to watch you have an argument. I'm not talking about little disagreements—these are normal, and to be expected in any studio recording session. I am talking about major philosophical differences. If one girl still thinks your band is death metal and the rest of you think it is rock, you should talk about that before starting to record your demo.

In addition to "creative differences" that can arise between bandmates there can also be personality differences. Let's say, for example, that you have a band of three girls. Three can be a magical number. It can also be a difficult one—two girls ganging up on the other, one girl feeling left out; two girls butting heads and arguing, one girl left in the middle trying to negotiate. These are just some examples of the dynamics that can—and most likely will—arise with a group of three.

Northern State is a band made up of three women with three very different personalities, tastes, styles, and ideas. We are close friends whose unique feelings and history tie in to our friendship, dreams, and aspirations. All of this background is rolled into the band we formed together—which is really a business we started when we were much younger than we are now. We have found ourselves in this marriage or partnership for almost eight years.

TEN POSITIVE THINGS TO LOVE
ABOUT YOUR BANDMATES

1. They are creative and have great ideas.
2. They make you laugh.
3. They help you laugh at yourself.
4. They are talented musicians.
5. They work hard and are always getting better.
6. They have great style.
7. They are each unique individuals who dare to be different.
8. They bring yummy snacks to rehearsal.
9. They know when it's time to talk.
10. They know when it's time to rock.

TEN THINGS YOUR BANDMATES
MIGHT DO THAT DRIVE YOU CRAZY

1. Show up late.
2. Show up unprepared (no music, no instrument, not ready to play).
3. Talk too much when it's time to rock.
4. Get bossy at rehearsals or meetings.
5. Not answer e-mails in a timely or complete fashion.
6. Answer e-mails out of order, or before reading the complete thread to find out the whole story (I love you, Spero!).
7. Screen their phone calls.
8. Make scheduling difficult.
9. Cancel or reschedule rehearsals.
10. Forget they have made commitments to the band.

From day one, it has not been easy. We have disagreed, argued, fought, not spoken, made up, been the best of friends, been the worst of enemies, and at times inspired, resented, learned from, been there for, connected with, and disappointed one another. We've experienced the highest of highs: our first gig, first interview, first great review, first recording session, first fan mail, first autograph, first recording, first television appearance, radio appearance, photo shoot, tour around the country, and then the world. We've opened for bands we have loved and admired since we were little girls. We have signed a record contract with a major label. We made a record with producers we respected. We stayed in fancy hotels and ordered room service by the pool. We have also shared the lowest of lows: the disappointment of not selling more records, leaving our major label, parting ways with people we loved working with because we could no longer pay them, and wondering if we made the right choices.

‹‹ TIP ››

Your band should feel like a group of girls with one strong voice and a clear message or purpose. This will hope-fully develop over time, through your experiences together. Scheduling fun band activities outside of or in addition to rehearsals is one way to help foster this feeling of camaraderie.

We have picked up the pieces and gotten back on our horse after falling off. We returned to the studio to write new songs, experiment musically, and inspire one another again.

At times, being in a band can feel like a roller-coaster ride, but remember that you have chosen to get on it with your bandmates, who are your friends and your girls. Do yourselves a favor and be patient with one another. Listen more until the moment comes to speak. Think about other people's ideas and take time to mull things over before you react. Keep the lines of communication open. Be as honest and forthright as you can without being bossy and pushy. Be who you are and express yourself creatively, but don't stifle the creativity of those around you. Try to let the creative process flow through you. Let one another's ideas bounce around the room and take shape, and be a good facilitator of other people's ideas. If that is not your strength, let someone else take on that role. Be open, loving, kind, and respectful. Do not shoot down other people's ideas, just as you would not like your own ideas shot down. A band is an exercise in dynamics that can take a long time to establish. It is just as difficult as any other relationship. It takes work, patience, respect, and compromise. No one person can call all the shots, unless you have started a one-woman band.

> *There have been times* when guys have come up to me and said, 'Wow, I usually don't like bands with chick singers, but you guys are really good.' While it sucks that some guys think that way, it feels good knowing that I'm helping to break down that barrier.

—COLLETTE MCLAFFERTY, *EDIBLERED*

Being GIRLS in a BOYS' World

At some point, you are going to look around—whether in a rehearsal space, at a gig, or in a recording studio—and find that you are the only girls within what feels like a five-hundred-mile radius. This is not uncommon at all in the music industry. At all levels, from the local music shop to gigs, rehearsal spaces, and recording studios—you will probably be in the minority of girls in a very male-centric world.

It is not always easy to deal with being in the minority, and it can often be intimidating and overwhelming. You may learn firsthand about being discriminated against because you are female, or feeling like you're not being taken seriously or being made to feel foolish. Sadly, most female musicians have a story to tell about some sound guy in some club who made them feel alienated.

The *good* news is that the more of us there are out there, the less likely this kind of behavior and treatment will continue. Each one of us who picks up an instrument and walks onto a stage, or into a recording booth, or practices at home in front of a mirror, is doing something revolutionary. We are all helping to move things forward for womankind and making it that much easier for the girls who come after us. No matter what kind of music you make, if you are rocking with an open mind and an open heart, you are part of a band of women and girls who believe in their right to rock.

Facing TEMPTATIONS Along the WAY

The main temptation bands face in the early stages is the allure of becoming huge stars overnight. Let me tell you, if you want to be a real band, with real fans, and real music that you write and play yourselves—it is simply not going to happen. Anyone who tells you it can is probably looking to make a quick buck by selling you some kind of service they will say you need in order to be successful. None of that works, I promise. You will pay money for things you think you need, and you will look back later and wish you had that money back for more important things. There is no way to become an overnight success. Nor should that be your goal.

Bands that have one huge hit song on the radio (one-hit wonders) end up fading into obscurity or becoming the punch line of bad jokes on VH1. If you want to have a career as a musician, and play in bands professionally, you have to start small and slowly work your way up. It is hard work, and often not very rewarding. However, it can be well worth resisting the temptations.

One offer you may get involves paying a lawyer to be put on "retainer" so he or she will help "shop" your record or band to different record companies and help you get a deal. Been there, done that. Highway robbery. Even if it's a big fancy entertainment lawyer in a fancy New York

office with gold records everywhere and phone calls coming in from record company executives while you are in the office, and even if he or she seems enthralled with your band and convinced you are going to be huge stars, *do not write out a check for anything.* Let him or her shop your band for free. If the lawyer does, indeed, find you some kind of record deal, he or she will make money by taking a percentage of your record advance. Such people do not need your $500 retainer, or whatever they ask for. Writing that check (or having your parents write it) is like kissing that money goodbye. Chances are, once you leave that office the lawyer will let your CD and press kit—the one you worked so hard to put together—gather dust on his or her desk, only to eventually put it in the circular file, otherwise known as the trash.

Another offer that might come your way involves a so-called "development deal." This one is about how a record company "discovers" a young band and wants the band to sign a contract agreeing to allow the record company to put out the band's records at some point in the future. A development deal implies that the artist or band is not yet ready to put out a record. Maybe they are too young, or inexperienced, or both. The record company might promise to help the young band hone their skills, work with top producers to write more "radio friendly" songs, polish their look and sound so they are ready for television, or any other number of attractive offers.

If you are not ready to put a record out into the world, what do you need a record label for? The same goes for hiring a manager and a lawyer. If what you need is time to develop as an artist, then do so. Keep playing music and writing songs and rehearsing with your band. If there are people you meet along the way who want to help you, and you feel they have something to teach you, then it might be an opportunity worth taking. But I urge you to avoid signing deals with anyone for a good, long while. If you do, you run the risk of never allowing yourself to develop naturally as an artist. It is better to let your music, your sound, and your image evolve based on creative expression and collaboration with your bandmates and other musicians. Once a label is introduced, those ideas can be clouded by what a particular record executive finds important, or thinks might help sell records in the future. You might also find that a record label signs you and then never puts out any records of yours at all! They could decide to put your project on the shelf and concentrate instead on another new, young, hip band that is *sure* to become famous overnight!

Rather than placing all your eggs in the baskets of people who promise things they will probably never deliver, focus on improving your musical skills, pushing the envelope with the songs you write and play, refining your image, and marketing yourself through visual media (website, videos, electronic press kit [EPK], flyers, banners, merch, local press, and so on). Over time, you will slowly and steadily build up a loyal group of fans who like your music and want to see you succeed. They will buy your music and merchandise, come see you play live, tell their friends about you, post your music on their MySpace page and blogs, pass out flyers or hang up posters for your shows and, in general, spread the word about who you are and what you do little by little, one person at a time. With this model, you can pave the way to a successful career in music, if that is what you choose.

The best reputation a musician can have is to be hardworking, tenacious, and determined. Playing in bands throughout your life that people love and respect can only help you when and if you try to make it big. As the music industry changes, the one thing that remains constant is the need for bands to have loyal fans to support them. You want the kind of "street cred" (or credibility) that is earned from hard work and years of rocking, despite all the challenges.

WHAT'S NEXT?

Taking Your Band to the Next Level

So, let's assume that you totally rock. Your band kicks butt, everyone loves you, you pack the room every time you play, your mailing list is growing steadily, you have fifteen thousand friends on MySpace, and every time you make a new piece of merch you sell out and keep adding more and more money to the band "account" (aka, the envelope in your sock drawer). Where do you go from here? How can you advance this project beyond your school and town? In this chapter we will explore what can happen above and beyond the local scene.

There are lots of resources available to help your band gain even more recognition. The first thing you have going for you is that you are different. Female bands still stand out in a sea of millions of dudes playing instruments. Girl groups are often viewed as a novelty, but if a group of girls can hold it down onstage and play solid music to an ever-growing legion of fans, they have the advantage of looking and sounding different from all the boy bands out there. You have every right in the world to be making music, and no one—and nothing—should stop you.

Since the beginning of Northern State there have been plenty of roadblocks laid down in our path that could have potentially dissuaded us from continuing. However, no matter what challenges have presented themselves, we have somehow managed to stay focused and continued to push our band to the next level. One of the more crucial moments came after our second record, *All City,* came out on Columbia Records. Before Columbia, we had been struggling as an independent band. Signing a record deal with a major label was incredibly exciting, and we jumped into the thrilling process of recording *All City* with, at least, some financial backing. Once the record was completed, however, we found ourselves removed from the decision-making process regarding what would happen to the record and where and how it would be sold. We were selling fewer records with Columbia's help than we had on our own and felt very frustrated with the major-label system.

That was definitely a moment when we could have given up and moved on with our lives. Instead, we went back into the studio and started making a new record—with no money and no plans for putting it out. It was awesome to take back control of our band and our career and to start the creative process anew. We knew that if we had fun making a new record, our fans would want to hear it and that we'd figure out a way to distribute it.

When the record was done, we signed with a much smaller, more artist-friendly label called Ipecac Recordings. We found it exciting to be part of a team working to promote our record and our band all over the country—and even the world. When our latest record, *Can I Keep This Pen?,* was released, Ipecac arranged for a window display at the Virgin Mega Store at Union Square in Manhattan. It was pretty exciting to walk down the street and see a giant picture of the cover of our album right at eye level, in the middle of Union Square. Since then, we have been touring consistently for almost a full year. We have been opening for Tegan & Sara in the United States, Canada, and all over Northern Europe, to sold-out audiences in every city, and returning to most markets on our own—to build on our fan base and play smaller, more intimate shows for lower ticket prices. It has been an amazing year filled with experiences I will never forget—not to mention lots of laughs with my two best girls. I can only imagine where this journey will take us next.

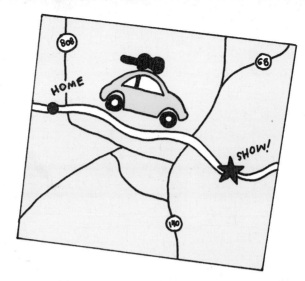

Choosing YOUR Next STEP

If the gigs you are playing in your local community are going well, it might be time to play a little farther away—in the next town, or nearest city. In the industry, a show played outside your hometown, and that is not connected to a tour, is called a *one-off*. (Once you are on the road and playing a few shows along the route, you are *on tour.*)

There are lots of things to consider when playing a one-off. For example, will you make enough money at the gig to cover the cost of getting to the venue and staying overnight, if necessary? You may be able to get a "guarantee" from the venue. If they guarantee to pay you, say, $100—is that enough money to reimburse a parent or friend to drive the band (and gear) and pay for parking (if necessary) and any other expenses? And what if it isn't enough—does that mean you shouldn't book the gig?

At the beginning of every band's career, not every show is a money-making venture. In many cases, the goal is simply to "break even," or not *lose* money. If you can cover your expenses, and you get to play in a new town and share your music with a new audience, then consider the gig a success. If you have merch or a demo, EP, or LP to sell, bring it and set up a merchandise table at the gig. The money you earn in sales can be considered part of the money earned at the gig. If there are any profits left over after expenses, you can decide as a band whether you want to split them, or reinvest them back into the band for new merch, a recording of new songs, or new gear.

If your live gigs are going great but you haven't yet recorded a demo or EP, you might consider saving money from the gigs and planning some kind of recording. If you have already recorded a demo or EP, think about recording a full-length LP. You can re-record some songs from your demo or EP, or start fresh with new material. Remember to review chapter 15 for your options, and be ready to spend your money wisely. The key to taking advantage of studio time is to do as much pre-production work as possible. Have your songs written and rehearsed so that you know what you want to accomplish when you are in the recording studio.

Making AN *Electronic Press Kit*

Another tool helpful in spreading the word about your band is an electronic press kit, or EPK. An EPK is a short video made up of live footage, interviews, snippets of music videos, and candid shots of the band. Its purpose is to give viewers a taste of what your band is all about—what you look like, how you sound, and who you are as personalities. Try to appear relaxed in front of the camera, acting natural and talking about your band, the music you write, your fans, and anything else.

If you are looking to book gigs in other towns but are having difficulty, an EPK could convince someone to hire you for their event or party, or get you accepted to some kind of talent showcase. More than just sending a demo of a few recorded songs, an EPK gives someone who has never seen or heard your band a better idea of what you are all about. Seeing what you look like, hearing your music, and getting a sense of what you are like as people can help outsiders feel connected to your project and inspire them to help move you forward. It could be someone in a position to book your band for a gig, write about your band in a local paper, or even a record or publishing company that might be interested in investing money in your project, or promoting you in some other way.

Our crowd snowballed rather quickly and enthusiastically, and the support and joyful exchange of our audience to our band eased us into a full-time musician's life in the local scene in Dallas. Then we were lucky enough to be heard by an A&R [artists and repertoire] person and referred to Geffen records.

—EDIE BRICKELL, *EDIE BRICKELL & THE NEW BOHEMIANS*

Getting written about in Time Out New York and The Village Voice was instrumental in moving us forward—never underestimate the power of local press! —SPERO, *NORTHERN STATE*

Depending on the level of professionalism you want, this is something you can do yourselves, or with a more experienced videographer. If you pay someone to make your EPK, make sure you feel comfortable with the arrangement and that you will have a say in the final editing process. The last thing you want is to spend the money your band has saved to make an EPK that does not represent your band accurately, or as you had intended.

Making an EPK yourselves will help you to avoid these problems. If you have a digital video camera, you are already ahead of the game. If not, perhaps you have a friend who will loan one to you, or know someone who is interested in filmmaking and wants to help put the video together. The EPK should not be too long, and there are a number of free (or inexpensive) editing programs you can use on your computer. If you have a Mac, iMovie is probably the easiest to use. You can add MP3s of your music as background for the piece, or for the intro or ending. If you have already made a music video, you can add footage from that as well.

𝒯𝒽𝑒 LETTER 𝑜𝑓 𝑡𝒽𝑒 LAW

Have you written songs that people have really responded to? There are many songwriting competitions you can enter to win cash prizes or publishing deals. Before you do anything like that, however, you might want to get your songs copyrighted.

Copyright is legal protection for any kind of written or artistic expression. Copyright laws give the creator (in this case, you) the exclusive right to copy, share, perform, and display the work for others. This means no one else can use it, copy it, or perform it without your permission.

◀◀ TIP ▶▶

Throughout your band's career, take time every so often to think about how things are going with your own personal playing. Have you been steadily rehearsing and practicing on your own? Are you improving and feeling more confident with your instrument? Are you still taking lessons? Is it time to consider other avenues to showcase your talents, such as in a jazz combo or vocal group?

If you are interested in copyrighting your music, it is not difficult to write out the melodies and print lyrics, fill out the necessary forms, and send them to the copyright office. There are plenty of websites that will help you with the process and explain reasons for doing so (or not doing so).

Another legal process you might want to consider at some point is incorporating your band as an official business. This is mostly for tax purposes. If your band starts making a lot of money—especially if you start playing in situations where you get paid with a check—you will need a bank account into which to deposit the money. Once that happens, if it's over a certain amount, you will be sent a W9 at the end of the year to pay taxes on the amount of money your band was paid. There are plenty of websites and resource books out there with more information about the benefits of incorporating your band and information on how to do so.

After THE *Band...*

Sooner or later, your band is going to face the inevitable. What happens when you all move away, maybe to attend college, like at the end of the movie *Grease*? Are the days of your first band coming to an end? If they are, it's okay. In fact, it's recommended. You have a whole future of starting and playing in bands, and you already have more experience than most people your age.

That said, this might be a good time to reevaluate your personal, music-related goals. How serious are you about music? Are you interested in a college-level music program, or even a conservatory where you can study voice, arranging, or a musical instrument in more depth?

Or, perhaps you found a particular aspect of the music industry interesting and want to consider a career on the other side. Was recording in the studio the most fascinating part for you? Maybe you'd enjoy audio engineering and recording other bands for a living. Business classes and law school can prepare you for careers as an entertainment lawyer, band manager, producer, or record label owner.

Even if you decide to get a liberal arts education and then go to medical school to become a neurosurgeon, the classes you take will help you later in life if you decide to continue playing in bands as a hobby. There is no amount of learning that can't help prepare you for the road ahead. Plus, being a college-educated woman in the music industry does give you a leg up on the competition. Understanding record deals, how publishing works, and what goes on in the recording studio are all useful things to know for anyone intending to pursue a career in, or relating to, the music industry.

In the early years of our band, when we were in our early twenties, whenever Northern State went in for some kind of meeting with record company executives, lawyers, or agents, the people we met with were always impressed with the way we presented ourselves. We tried to be as informed and educated as possible about the situation we were entering into. Similar to what happens during a job interview, before a record company is going to invest any money in your band, or a lawyer do any work for you, or an agent consider booking any paying gigs for you, they will all want to know whether you are a professional act that is taking its business seriously and that can be trusted and relied upon.

Ultimately, the purpose of starting a band is determined by each of its individual members. There is no magic formula to follow, no recipe for success. The best advice I can give you is to find a fun group of girls who inspire you and make you laugh. Get together and experiment with playing music, writing songs, and developing some kind of band image. Remember that you are not locked into this particular group or style of music forever. Your creativity and talents are only just beginning to emerge. Have fun with it and push yourself to learn more, to master your instrument, and to be the girl who knows about the gear.

Get out there and rock.

FIVE WAYS BEING IN A BAND HELPS PREPARE YOU FOR THE FUTURE

1. Being in a band helps to build confidence for any kind of career that involves getting up in front of large groups of people, be it teaching, public speaking, lecturing, or some other kind of performance.
2. Being in a band can help teach financial independence, business savvy, budgeting, and dealing with overall money management.
3. Being in a band helps improve interpersonal relationships and helps each member become better at communication, negotiation, and mediation.
4. Being in a band can introduce you to legal contracts and agreements, and the importance of learning how to read the fine print . . .
5. Being in a band helps teach time management, organizational skills, how to deal with scheduling, as well as planning for the future.

Talking the Talk: A GLOSSARY

The following definitions are here to help you understand certain terms that are used throughout this book. Some of the entries are more formal, while others are meant to explain certain lingo you'll hear in the business.

¼-INCH CABLE: Cable that fits into ¼-inch connections and is used to plug guitars, basses, and keyboards into amplifiers.

A CAPPELLA: A vocal part without any instruments accompanying it.

ACOUSTICS: The sound quality of a space or venue; how well or poorly it conveys and reflects sound waves to be heard by the audience.

ADAPTOR: A device that attaches to the end of a cable to change its shape or size so that it can be properly plugged into the desired input (opening).

ADVANCING THE SHOW: The act of calling ahead a few weeks prior to a gig to establish contact with someone at the venue and arrange the details of the event.

ALLITERATION: The repetition of usually initial consonant sounds in two or more neighboring words or syllables (as in "wild and woolly," "threatening throngs"); also called head rhyme or initial rhyme.

AMP: Short for "amplifier"; a piece of equipment you plug into an instrument to increase its volume. There are combo amps and amps that come in two pieces—the head and the cabinet. You attach the head to the speaker cabinet (or "cab") using a ¼-inch cable.

AUDIO OR SOUND ENGINEER: The person who sits behind "the boards" and actually records your band, or mixes the sound live during a performance.

BACKING OR BACKUP VOCALS: Background singers who usually sing in harmony with the lead vocalist, other backing vocalists, or alone, but who do not sing the lead. They may also perform certain moves, or dance onstage to the music.

BALANCE: Equality of volume on a recording or during a live performance.

BAND MANAGER: One who guides the career of artists in the entertainment business. His or her responsibility is to oversee the day-to-day business affairs of an artist and to advise clients about professional and personal decisions that may affect their career.

BASSIST: One who plays the bass guitar. Basses are stringed instruments similar in design to the guitar but with a longer scale and tuned to a lower pitch. Electric basses are amplified and played through a speaker (or amp).

BIO: Biography, which your band can place on a website, press kit, or on a CD or demo of your music for wide distribution.

BLOG: Web log, which is a home base or forum on the Internet for your band or other interests. It allows for exchange of ideas with others online and can be a place you can promote your band's music and activities.

BOOKING AGENT: The person who finds jobs or gigs for musicians, bands, artists, and other people in the entertainment business. Agents make their money by taking a percentage of what their client is paid.

BRIDGE: A musical passage linking two sections of a composition.

BUYOUT: A stipend that covers the cost of meals for band members playing at a gig.

CADENCE: A rhythmic sequence or flow of sounds in a piece of music. Also, a sequence of chords or a vocal line that is moving to a harmonic resolution.

CANS: Headphones you wear during a recording session.

CD: Compact disc.

CHANNEL: The inputs used in a soundboard or mixing console. In a PA system, you will need at least as many inputs/channels as microphones you plan to use.

CHORD: A combination of musical tones that are played at the same time.

CHORUS: The main part of a popular song. It regularly repeats, and can be the "hook" for that piece.

COMBO AMP: An all-in-one unit made up of speaker cabinet, and head (with all the necessary knobs, plugs, and dials) that is more portable than an amp that comes in two or more parts.

COMP: To compile; done by the studio engineer and producer who are recording or mixing your record. He or she will compile the takes so you have the best possible sound on every note.

CONSUMABLES: Items for playing music that you'll need to replace when they wear out, such as guitar strings, picks (plectrums), drumheads, and drumsticks.

CONTROL ROOM: The room in which the engineer and producer control the recording.

COPYRIGHT: Legal protection for any kind of artistic expression. Copyright laws give the creator the sole right to copy, share, perform, and display the work. No one else can do so without the artist's permission.

COVER: Also known as cover version, cover song, or simply cover, a new rendition (performance or recording) of a previously recorded song. Also refers to the act of performing someone else's song live.

CURFEW: At a venue, the time at which everything needs to be finished for closing.

DEMO: Short for *demonstration*; a brief sample of your band's music, burned onto a CD or shared via an MP3 file, to promote your group. The demo can be recorded in a studio or at home with your own equipment, such as a four-track recorder.

DI BOX OR DI UNIT: DI stands for "direct input," "direct injection," or "direct interface." These electronic devices are used to plug certain instruments and microphones into a PA system, usually used onstage.

DOWNLOADABLE TRACKS: A method for sharing your music online. Listeners can save your songs as MP3 files using their computer and iPod or other portable music player.

DRUM KEY: A type of wrench for tightening the special screws or lugs used on the drums to attach the heads to the drum hoops.

DRUM KIT OR SET: A complete drum kit includes snare, kick, floor tom, rack tom, high hat, crash cymbal, ride cymbal, and drum throne (or stool).

DRUMHEAD: The membrane stretched over one or both open ends of a drum. When the head is struck with drumsticks, mallets, or hands, it vibrates, causing sound to resonate.

DRUMMER: Person who plays the drums and/or percussion instruments; sometimes known as the percussionist.

DVD: Digital video disc. It can contain audio and visual information and be played on a computer or DVD player.

DYNAMICS: The loudness or softness of a passage of music within a song and how these qualities change throughout the whole piece.

ELECTRIC GUITAR: Vibrations of metal strings create electrical signals in electromagnetic sensors called pickups. The signals are then amplified (made louder) and played through a speaker.

ELECTRONIC PRESS KIT: EPK for short, this promotional piece is a short video

made up of live footage, interviews, snippets of music videos, and candid shots of the band.

E-MAIL LIST: An ongoing collection of the names and addresses of your fans, taken from the Internet through your band's website or blog, or from fans signing up at shows.

EP: Stands for "extended play"; describes vinyl records or CDs that contain more than one single but are too short to qualify as long-playing (LP) albums. Usually contains four to seven tracks; such recordings are ten to twenty-five minutes long.

FAN BASE: All your potential audience and supporters. You build up your base through collecting mailing lists, friends, family, and other contacts.

FOLK: Traditional acoustic (rather than electric) music. Its roots are in country-and-western, blues, gospel, Celtic music, and bluegrass.

FOUR-TRACK: A small-scale recording mixing board that you can use at home to make professional-sounding records. It allows you to record four different tracks of music or vocals.

FREE WRITING, OR STREAM OF CONSCIOUSNESS: Putting down your thoughts on paper fluidly, without thinking too much, as in a journal or notebook. This type of exercise can become the raw material for songs, poems, or other artworks.

FRONT PERSON: The person who stands (or sits) up front onstage and interacts with the audience the most—can be the lead vocalist, lead guitarist, rhythm guitarist, keyboard player, bass player, drummer, or secondary vocalist. In rap music, the lead vocalist is known as the MC (or emcee).

GEAR HEAD: Someone who knows a lot about equipment, likes to use it, study it, and acquire it.

GRAPHIC DESIGNER: Someone who assembles images, words, or motion graphics to create an artwork for published, printed, or electronic media, such as brochures and advertising.

Graphic designers can also do typesetting, illustration, and Web design.

GUARANTEE: The minimum amount that the band will be paid. Does not include extras such as merchandise sales.

GUEST LIST: A limited roster of names that the band compiles of guests who do not have to pay to attend the gig.

HARMONIES: Secondary melodies that blend well with the main melody line. These can be sung by backup vocalists or played on instruments.

HEADLINER: The main act performing in a show, preceded by one or more opening acts.

HIP-HOP: A genre of music, fashion, and urban culture. Hip-hop vocals usually consists of a rhythmic style of speech called "rap." The words are spoken over backup beats, which used to be performed on a turntable by a DJ, but are now often played on instruments or rhythm machines. Graffiti art and break dancing are also part of hip-hop.

HOOK: A device, especially in music or writing that catches the attention.

HOUSE: The room or space in which the music is being played at a live venue.

IMAGERY: Description involving the five senses (sight, touch, hearing, taste, and smell). Similes and metaphors can be used in songwriting to create vivid images, as though you were painting a picture with words and music.

INPUTS: Also referred to as "ins," the $1/4$-inch or XLR openings in a mixing console, PA system, four-track, etc., into which you plug an instrument, microphone, or amp.

INTRO: A musical passage or section that opens a movement or song.

JAMMING: To take part in a jam session, an often spontaneous performance by a group (especially of jazz musicians) that is improvising on various musical themes.

JPEG: A graphic file format that allows you to share your files, visual or music, and to upload or download them more easily.

KEYBOARDIST: Person who plays the piano, electric piano, synthesizer, or other keyboard instrument.

LEAD GUITARIST: One who performs melodies, counter-melodies, and solos.

LEAD SINGER: The front person who performs the main vocals of a song.

LIVE ROOM: A soundproof room in which instruments are recorded.

LIVE: Playing in front of an audience, as opposed to recording in a studio or other closed setting.

LOAD-IN: The time the band needs to arrive in order to set up gear in a venue.

LOGO: The graphic design symbol, possibly combined with words, that stands for your band and can be reproduced on your merchandise and other items.

LP: Refers to "long playing," from when music was released on LP vinyl records. In digital music, it usually means an album that has eight or more tracks and is between twenty-five and eighty minutes long.

LYRICS: The words of a song.

MASTERING: Once the mixing is finished, mastering prepares the music so it is ready for production as CDs, MP3s, or vinyl.

MC: Master of ceremonies, who performs lead vocals in rap and hip-hop music, using spoken, rhythmic lyrics, or improvisation. Also spelled "emcee."

MELODY LINE: A series of notes arranged into a musical phrase. The main theme of a song, onto which harmonies and instrumental parts are added.

MERCH: Short for merchandise; any salable items you offer at shows and elsewhere, including T-shirts, CDs, videos, and posters, in order to promote your band.

MERCHANDISE SPLIT: At a gig, the percentage of the proceeds from the merchandise you sell, and the portion given to the house. A common split is 85% for the band and 15% for the venue.

METAL: An offshoot of hard rock that has an intense and loud guitar part. It adds feedback, distortion, and driving rhythms to its sound, along with a bad attitude.

MICROPHONE: A handheld device for amplifying sound using electric current. Also referred to as mic (pronounced mike).

MIXING BOARD: The board in a studio's control room with all the recording equipment and controls. A type of "nerve center," it contains inputs connected by cables, and various channels for recording multiple tracks.

MIXING: The process during which the levels are set for the various instrumental parts and vocals you recorded, like volume, frequency, and dynamics. Once a recording is finished, sound effects can be added and adjusted.

MONITOR MIX: The balance of sound coming from the PA system's extra speakers that the performers onstage can hear. It may be different from the audience's experience of the mix.

MONITORS: Extra speakers connected to the PA system so that band members can hear the vocals and other instruments more clearly.

MP3: A digital file format into which you may want to convert your track in order to upload it onto a website or download it to listen to it on an MP3 player.

MUSICAL BREAK: A place in a song at which all instruments play together without vocals.

NOTE: A written symbol on a musical staff. It shows the length and pitch of a tone by its shape and position.

ONE-OFF: A single show, played outside of one's hometown, which is not part of a tour.

ONOMATOPOEIA: A vocal imitation of the sound associated with a thing or action. Its name could be similar to the sound it makes, such as whirr, pop, or hum.

OPENER: The band that opens for the lead, or headline act. They play the initial set and warm up the audience for the main part of the show.

OUTPUT: The signal coming out of an instrument, amplifier, mixer, etc.

OUTRO: Combines the words "out" and "intro"; in popular music, usually denotes the concluding lines of a song. The equivalent in classical music is the coda, and the traditional term is tag.

P&D DEAL: Production and distribution of a demo recording or full record. A company manufactures and produces copies of your record and then distributes the copies to specialty record stores.

PA SYSTEM: Short for "public address system"; used to amplify vocal microphones and other devices or instruments that one is not plugging directly into an amp.

POETRY: The basis for much songwriting, especially in folk music and hip-hop. Its rhyme scheme, alliteration, onomatopoeia, voice, tempo, cadence, structure, tone, and imagery can be set to music.

PORTMANTEAU: A word that is created by blending two other words together, for example, "blog," which combines the words Web and log.

PRE-PRODUCTION: Time spent writing and rehearsing songs before going into the studio to record. The planning stage that will decide how you want your recordings to sound.

PRODUCER: Person who works with the band to help make recording decisions and who oversees the recording process, sometimes adding his or her own creative insights.

PROGRESSION: A succession of musical tones or chords.

PROMOTER: A person or company in the business of marketing and promoting concerts, festivals, and other live entertainment events.

PUBLICIST: A person whose job it is to

create and manage press or communications for a public figure, celebrity, or artist with a positive "spin" (emphasis).

PUNCH IN: A select re-recording of part of a track or song by a studio sound engineer.

PUNK: A type (genre) of rock that is faster, wilder, and more hard-driving than other rock music, with shorter, brasher songs. Later called alternative rock. The movement began in the 1970s in the United States, Australia, and the United Kingdom.

RAP: Rapping is a vocal style in which the performer speaks in rhythm and often in rhyme, generally to a beat. The main rapper is called the MC (or emcee). Beats are taken from parts of other songs, made using synthesizers, drum machines, or live bands. Rappers may perform their own poetry or improvise rhyming lyrics while onstage, which is known as free-styling.

REFRAIN: Musical theme or verse that repeats at intervals in a song. Often a type of hook, or catchy melody, that is easy to remember.

RHYME SCHEME: The arrangement of rhymes in a stanza or a poem. For example, AABB or ABAB.

RHYTHM GUITARIST: Provides the pulse or rhythm for a song, and harmonies that support the other instruments or voices.

RHYTHM: The pulse, beat, accent, and tempo of a piece that keep it moving forward.

ROCK: Pop music that is known for its youthfulness, beat, electric instruments, rebellious energy, and catchy melodies, or "hooks."

SET: The list of songs a band or artist plans to play during a concert.

SINGLE: A recording that usually has one to three songs, up to about ten minutes in length. Or can refer to the song that is "released" to radio, and pushed with a video, etc.

SOLO: A featured instrumental or vocal part played alone that can be improvised or planned.

SONGWRITER: A member of the band or someone outside the group who creates and arranges new pieces for the group to perform, perhaps in collaboration with others.

SOUND CHECK: Before a concert or show, the band and sound crew run through a small portion of the upcoming set to make sure the sound in the venue is clear, with the right volume, balance, and tonal frequencies.

SOUND EFFECTS: Delay, reverb (reverberation), echo, panning, etc., which can be added to audio to enhance the original recording. It can also be used live onstage to change the sound of certain instruments.

SOUNDBOARD RECORDING: Recording your band playing live using a digital recording device. It can be plugged into the soundboard to get a mix that sounds exactly like what's coming out of the speakers at the show.

SOUNDPROOFING: Foam insulation, corkboard, or other material for attaching to walls to help them absorb sound and to protect the rest of a building from noise.

STREAMING AUDIO: A form of music sampled over the Internet. It allows the user to access all or parts of your band's songs using media software on their computer.

STREET CRED: Credibility, reputation.

SUBHOOK: Some songs include a second hook, or catchy theme, before or after the chorus as a lead-in or lead-out.

TALKBACK BUTTON: The button the producer/engineer uses to communicate with the musicians recording in the live room and/or vocal booth.

TALKING POINTS: Topics band members want to remember to mention in between songs during their set—from thanking people to introducing band members to promoting their merchandise and future concerts.

TEMPO: The rate of speed of a musical piece or passage. Organized by time signature, into counts and bars, such as 2/4, or 4/4 time.

TONE: A sound with a certain pitch and vibration. Could also be the style or manner of expression that is conveyed through music, speech, or writing.

TRACK: The number of songs being recorded or the number of instruments being recorded separately within a song. As a verb, meaning to record, possibly on a separate track (as in, "to track the drums").

UNPLUGGED: Acoustic-style music, played without amplification.

VERSE: Two or more sections of a song with basically the same music but having different lyrics.

VINYL: A vinyl record. If you are interested in having your music made into a vinyl record, you will need to have it mastered specifically for vinyl.

VOCAL BOOTH: A sound proof booth used to record vocals.

VOICE: A literary term used to describe the individual writing style of an author.

WIRELESS MICROPHONE: Cordless microphones that allow singers to move around freely onstage when performing live.

WRITE-UP: A piece written about your group, appearing in a newspaper, blog, or other medium, which can give your band good publicity.

XLR CABLES: Cables used with microphones that have "extra low resistance," meaning they transmit sound efficiently.

Rock Camp Resource Guide

In 2007, seven different rock camps specifically for girls came together and formed the Girls Rock Camp Alliance (www.girlsrockcamp.org). Northern State performed at one of the camps: the Willie Mae Camp for Girls, in Brooklyn, New York. And, although I am in no way affiliated with the organization, I think they are an awesome resource for up-to-date information on rock camps for girls. The Alliance is made up of rock camps for girls throughout the country and the world. Here are a few of the camps to check out:

Bay Area Girls Rock Camp (California)
WWW.BAYAREAGIRLSROCKCAMP.ORG

Girls Rock Camp (Austin, Texas)
PHONE: 512-809-7799
WWW.GIRLSROCKCAMPAUSTIN.ORG

Girls Rock! UK (London)
WWW.GIRLSROCKUK.ORG

Rock 'n' Roll Camp for Girls (Portland, Oregon)
PHONE: 503-445-4991
WWW.GIRLSROCKCAMP.ORG

Willie Mae Rock Camp for Girls (Brooklyn, New York)
PHONE: 212-777-1323
WWW.WILLIEMAEROCKCAMP.ORG

Plenty of other rock schools and summer camps have sprung up all over the country that are not affiliated with the Girls Rock Camp Alliance. Many of these are coed, meaning there are boys and girls rocking out alongside each other, many times in the same band! Here are a couple that Northern State has performed at and helped raise money for:

The Power Chord Academy (with locations all over the country)
WWW.POWERCHORDACADEMY.COM

The Paul Green School of Rock Music (with locations all over the country)
WWW.SCHOOLOFROCK.COM

And here are a few other resources to help you locate rock camps near you:

Kids Camps.com: Music Camps and Programs
WWW.KIDSCAMPS.COM/ART/MUSIC.HTML

My Summer Camps.com
WWW.MYSUMMERCAMPS.COM/CAMPS/ARTS_CAMPS/MUSIC/INDEX.HTML

Soundwall Music Rock Camp (Santa Cruz, California)
PHONE: 925-518-8289
WWW.ROCKCAMP.ORG

Acknowledgments: This book would not have been possible without the amazing Mark Shulman. Thank you for believing in me when you hardly knew me . . . and then for believing some more. Thank you to Julie Mazur, Cathy Hennessy, Andrea Glickson, and all the amazing people at Watson-Guptill and Billboard Books. Many thanks to Barbara Robbins for being a rockin' lawyer and reviewing my contract, Chris Hibbins for the rockin' technical seal of approval and to Tegan Quin and Sara Quin for believing in Northern State and giving us so many amazing opportunities. Major thanks to Edie Brickell and Kim Gordon for taking the time to write such inspiring words. To my dad, for rocking since before I was born; my brother Jeff, for starting a band first and inspiring me to start one myself; and my mom for putting up with all of it and encouraging me no matter what. To my cohorts in Northern State, Spero and Jules, for supporting the idea of me writing this book, and daring to live the dream with me; and for Jonathan Wynn, my cohort in life, for helping me with all things, teaching me to sit still and write, and for having the patience and understanding to love me, my family, and my band. And finally, to the greater NSP, who have supported me for the last eight years.